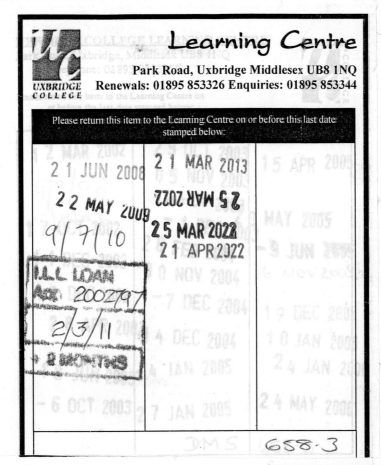

Learning Centre

Park Road, Uxbridge Middlesex UB8 1NQ
Renewals: 01895 853326 Enquiries: 01895 853344

UXBRIDGE COLLEGE

Please return this item to the Learning Centre on or before this last date stamped below:

2 MAR 2002
2 1 JUN 2008
2 2 MAY 2009
9/7/10

ILL LOAN
2002797
2/3/11
8 MONTHS

- 6 OCT 2003

2 1 MAR 2013
25 MAR 2022
25 MAR 2022
2 1 APR 2022
0 NOV 2004
- 7 DEC 2004
4 DEC 2004
4 IAN 2005
7 JAN 2005

15 APR 2005
MAY 2005
- 9 JUN 2005
6 NOV 2005
1 9 DEC 2005
1 0 JAN 2006
2 4 JAN 2006
2 4 MAY 2006

DMS   658.3

Titles in the
TEAM LEADER DEVELOPMENT SERIES

Information Management

Sally Palmer

Head of Stockport College of Further and Higher Education Business School.

Margaret Weaver

Lecturer in Business Studies, Stockport College of Further and Higher Education. Fellow of Association of Chartered and Certified Accountants.

Information Management unlocks all the essential communication skills for today's supervisors and team leaders. It includes:
● presentation skills from OHPs to video conferencing.
● the supervisor's role in team briefings and feedback.
● a chapter on how to write a management project.

0 7506 3862 1: paperback: June 1998

People and Self Management

Sally Palmer

Head of Stockport College of Further and Higher Education Business School.

People and Self Management leads the reader through all the skills needed for today's supervisor/team leader, including:
● how to assess and improve your workplace performance.
● the essential skills of effective self management.
● the management of change.

0 7506 3861 3: paperback: June 1998

Resources Management

Margaret Weaver

Lecturer in Business Studies, Stockport College of Further and Higher Education. Fellow of Association of Chartered and Certified Accountants.

Resources Management is the absolute guide to all areas of resource control. It includes:
● thorough coverage of all areas of resource control for supervisors.
● clear explanations of theories and techniques of control.
● practical exercises to reinforce skills and knowledge.
● application of theory to the work-based problems facing today's managers.

0 7506 3863 X : paperback: June 1998

Activities Management

Cathy Lake

Freelance management writer.

Activities Management is a comprehensive guide to running a smooth and successful operation. It includes:
● practical help on how to plan and manage work.
● health and safety in the workplace.
● environmental considerations that today's supervisor needs to know.
● how to become a quality focussed organization

0 7506 4042 1: paperback: October 1998

People and Self
MANAGEMENT

Team Leader Development Series

Sally Palmer

OXFORD   BOSTON   JOHANNESBURG   MELBOURNE   NEW DELHI   SINGAPORE

Butterworth-Heinemann
Linacre House, Jordan Hill, Oxford OX2 8DP
225 Wildwood Avenue, Woburn, MA 01801–2041
A division of Reed Educational and Professional Publishing Ltd

 A member of the Reed Elsevier plc group

First published 1998

British Library Cataloguing in Publication Data
A catalogue record for this is available from the British Library

ISBN 0 7506 3861 3

Composition by Genesis Typesetting, Rochester, Kent
Printed and bound in Great Britain

Contents

5 Leading your team   **78**

6 Training and developing your team   **101**

12 Managing change   218

References   234

Further Reading   236

Index   237

Introduction

Introduction

There are four books in the Team Leader Development Series, *People and Self Management*, *Information Management*, *Resources Management* and *Activities Management*, covering key topics from the four principal roles of management. The series has been designed to provide you with the knowledge and skills needed to carry out the role of team leader. The actual name of the job role of a team leader will vary from organization to organization. In your organization, the job role might be called any of the following:

- team leader
- supervisor
- first line manager
- section leader
- junior manager
- chargehand
- foreman
- assistant manager
- administrator.

If you work in the services or a hospital, team leaders may be called by another name not on the above list. However, in this series 'team leader' has been used throughout to describe the job role.

Who the series is intended for

If you have line-management responsibility for people within your organization, or you are hoping to progress to a position in which you will have this responsibility, then this series is for you. You may have been recently promoted into a team leader position or you may have been a team leader for some time. The series is relevant for you whether you work in a small organization or a large organization, whether you work in the public sector, private sector or voluntary sector. The books are designed to provide you with practical help which will enable you to perform better at work and to provide support to a range of programmes of study which have been designed specifically for team leaders.

Related programmes of study

There are a number of management qualifications that have been designed for team leaders. The titles in this series have been structured around the four key roles of management: Managing People, Managing Activities, Managing Resources and Managing Information. The content of each title has been developed in accordance with all the main qualifications in this area. Your tutor, manager or trainer will help you design a programme of study for your particular qualification route. Further details about each syllabus can be found in the tutor supplement that accompanies this textbook.

People and Self Management covers the core topics in this key role of management detailed in the programmes of study from the National Examining Board of Supervision and Management, the Institute of Supervisory Management, Edexel and the Institute of Management who all award qualifications in Supervisory Management. The Team Leader Development Series has also been devised to provide material that is relevant for those who are working towards a NVQ or SVQ at level 3 in management. The national management standards at this level cover the full range of general management activities which all managers working in a team leader position are expected to carry out. The Team Leader Development Series covers all the core topics involved with the activities defined in each of the key roles of management listed above. Your tutor will have full details about the national standards.

The content of *People and Self Management* covers the essential underpinning knowledge for the following units:

C1   Manage oneself (*mandatory*)
C4   Create effective working relationships (*mandatory*)

C7   Contribute to the selection of personnel for activities (*mandatory*)

C9   Contribute to the development of teams and individuals (*optional*)

C12   Lead the work of teams and individuals to achieve their objectives (*optional*)

C15   Respond to poor performance in your team (*optional*)

These units of competence consist of the following elements:

C1.1   Develop your own skills to improve your performance

C1.2   Manage your time to meet your objectives

C4.1   Gain the trust and support of colleagues and team members

C4.2   Gain the trust and support of your manager

C4.3   Minimise conflict in your team

C7.1   Contribute to identifying personnel requirements

C7.2   Contribute to selecting required personnel

C9.1   Contribute to the identification of development needs

C9.2   Contribute to planning the development of teams and individuals

C9.3   Contribute to development activities

C9.4   Contribute to the assessment of people against development objectives

C12.1   Plan the work of teams and individuals

C12.2   Assess the work of teams and individuals

C12.3   Provide feedback to teams and individuals on their work

C15.1   Help team members who have problems affecting their performance

C15.2   Contribute to implementing disciplinary and grievance procedures

The work-based assignments, which can be used to gather evidence for your portfolio, are mapped to the relevant elements of competence so that you can see which elements you are working towards.

As part of your work towards a vocational qualification in management at level 3, you also have to demonstrate that you have developed a number of personal competencies (in other words, skills and attitudes) that will enable you to apply your knowledge and understanding to a range of different situations at work. You will cover the range of personal competencies in many aspects of your work. This book will be particularly helpful in providing support for the following personal competencies:

- acting assertively
- behaving ethically
- building teams
- focusing on results
- influencing others
- managing self
- thinking and taking decisions

Synopsis of *People and Self Management*

This book starts by looking at the role of a team leader and the factors that influence the way in which people behave at work. If you can improve your understanding of the way in which individuals behave, it will be easier to understand how to become a more effective team leader. The book then examines the organizations in which you work, and moves on to cover how you can effectively manage your workteam, by understanding how teams behave, how to select new team members and how to lead your team. The important aspects of developing your team, problem solving, decision making and handling conflict, including how to deal with grievance and disciplinary procedures are also covered. A whole chapter is devoted to managing change; this is because this is such an important aspect of a team leader's role in organizations today. Last, but certainly not least, this volume covers managing yourself including key aspects such as managing time, stress and your own workload. Assertiveness and planning for your own future development are also covered in this section.

Learning structure

Each chapter begins with **Learning objectives**, a list of statements which say what you will be able to do, after you have worked through the chapter. This is followed by the 'Introduction', a few lines which introduce the material that is covered in the chapter.

There are several **Activities** in each chapter. You will find the answers at the end of the book.

There are also **Investigates** in each chapter, these are related to something which has been covered in the text. The suggestion is that you investigate the matter that has just been covered in your own organization. It is important, that you understand what you have learned, but also that you can relate what you have learned to your own organization.

Each chapter has a **Summary**, the summary recaps the main points that have been covered in the chapter, it round of the knowledge and skill areas that have been covered in the main body of the chapter, before the text moves into a range of tasks that you can complete to consolidate your learning.

There are a set of **Review and discussion questions** following the summary. You answer these after you have worked through the chapter to check whether you have understood and remembered the information that you have just read. Answers and guidelines to these questions can be found in the tutor resource material.

You are provided with an opportunity to deal with the issues raised in the chapter that you have just read by analysing the **Case study**. The case study is a scenario based in the workplace and a chance to 'practice' how you might deal with a situation at work.

There is a **Work-based assignment** at the end of each chapter, these have been designed, so that if you complete the assignment, you will be able to apply the knowledge and skills that you have covered in the chapter in the workplace. The relevant units of competence are shown in the portfolio icon where applicable. These will be of use to you if you are studying towards an S/NVQ at Level 3 in management.

1 The job of a team leader

Learning objectives

On completion of this chapter you will be able to:

- describe the term 'team leader'
- describe the key managerial tasks that make up the job of a team leader
- appreciate the importance of setting smart objectives
- describe the organizational hierarchy of objectives and plans
- differentiate between different types of plans
- explain the planning cycle
- describe the benefits of planning
- describe the stages in organizing
- understand the importance of monitoring and controlling plans.

Introduction

As a team leader you will have first line responsibility for people within your organization. Many of you will not only be responsible for leading your team but also be involved in day-to-day operations, so you are not only involved in managing the team but also in making the product or delivering the service. Your role as a team leader means that you are part of the management team and so there are many managerial aspects to your job. You are at the front line of management and have a major responsibility for seeing that work is done by others. Team leaders are involved in supervisory management; you are the link between more senior managers and the operatives that work in the organization. You will probably have noticed that there are fewer layers of management in organizations these days. As this process of reducing the number of management levels has taken place, the team leader has taken on more responsibility. In this chapter we will examine the management elements of a team leader's role.

What team leaders do

As a team leader you are concerned with making sure the work is done. Your manager will give you the information you need about what you have to achieve and your job is to get the team organized to produce the work.

What do you think are the main activities of a team leader? Compare your answers to the key managerial functions shown in Figure 1.1.

Like all managers at every level within the organization you need to carry out key managerial functions. These are illustrated in Figure 1.1.

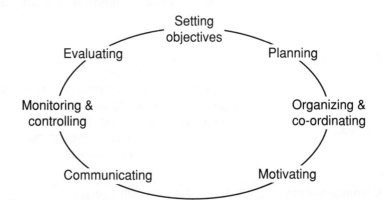

Figure 1.1
Managerial functions

Figure 1.2 gives more detail on each of the managerial functions as they apply to a team leader.

1 Setting objectives	As a team leader you must obtain clear objectives from your line manager and then agree and set objectives for your workteam. You need to check that the objectives are clearly communicated to your team and make plans to ensure that the objectives are achieved.
2 Planning	Objectives are where we want to get to. Plans are the means of getting there. It is the plans that calculate how to turn the objectives into reality. It is important to plan so that everybody knows what they have to do to achieve the objectives.
3 Organizing and coordinating	The activities of team members must be organized to ensure that everything runs smoothly and that problems are dealt with as they arise. Linked to organization is coordination; this is about coordinating everybody's efforts to make sure that the objectives are achieved. Also, your team will have to coordinate with other teams and departments within the organization.
4 Motivating	A team leader must ensure that the staff are motivated at work, that they are given opportunities to obtain job satisfaction and so are committed to the work of the organization and the team. This can be done by making sure that they are encouraged, developed, given responsibility and varied tasks, possibly through delegation; they will then feel valued by the organization.
5 Communicating	Keeping in touch with everything, keeping everybody informed about what is happening, listening to your team and consulting with your team.
6 Monitoring and controlling	When the objectives are clear, plans have been made for the achievement of the objectives, the work is organized and coordinated, the team leader must continue to be vigilant. Systems have to be put in place for monitoring progress against the plans, and control systems put in place so that if something is not going as planned it is picked up immediately by the team leader and corrective action is taken.
7 Evaluating	Evaluating is about appraising performance and assessing how you and your team are doing.

Figure 1.2 Managerial functions and the job of a team leader

Activity 2

Consider your job as a team leader and complete the table below.

Managerial element	Example of an activity carried out by me, in my role as a team leader in my organization, that demonstrates that this is part of a team leader's role
1 Setting objectives	
2 Planning	
3 Organizing and coordinating	
4 Motivating	
5 Communicating	
6 Monitoring and controlling	
7 Evaluating	

We will now look at each one of these key functions in more detail.

Setting objectives

You need to obtain clear objectives from your line manager. If your team is to perform well, you will need to agree and set objectives with your workteam. Setting objectives involves three main stages:

- clarifying the overall purpose of the team
- identifying the objectives that will have to be achieved by the team in order to achieve the overall purpose
- deciding what tasks will have to be completed to achieve the team objectives and purpose.

Your job is to is to clarify the team purpose and set clear objectives. You will need to keep a record of performance against the objectives which will help you to monitor the situation and keep your team and your line manager informed of progress.

Good objectives are SMART:

- **Specific** – everybody needs to know what has to be achieved. It is better if each objective consists of a single idea.
- **Measurable** – you need to consider how to measure the objective so that you will know how successful you have been.
- **Achievable** – objectives should stretch and develop the team members and yet be achievable.
- **Realistic** – the objective needs to be realistic; you can ensure this by using information to assess what has been achieved in the past and to predict what is realistic for the future.
- **Timed** – you need to be clear about the timescale within which the objective should be achieved.

(See *Activities Management*, Chapter 2, for more details.)

Planning

Objectives are where we want to get to; plans are the means of getting there. Plans show how you are going to turn the objectives into reality. Planning will help to ensure that the organizational and team objectives are achieved. Good planning means that everybody knows what they have to do to achieve the objectives. Good planning is essential for personal and organizational effectiveness. Planning is the most basic and probably the most important management function. Organizing, monitoring and controlling are linked to good planning. Organization and coordination turn plans into action, and monitoring and controlling keep plans on course.

Planning is about designing future action to cope with forecast situations. Planning sets down a course of action that gets us from where we are now, to where we want to be.

Plans are a management tool; once they are written down it would be a mistake to consider them to be fixed; as things are changing all the time, we might have to change our plans. It is, however, important to set them down even if we do not always stick to them, because they provide a sense of purpose, a direction in which we are travelling. In essence, planning is establishing a course of action.

Figure 1.3
The organizational hierarchy of objectives and plans. The exact way in which the hierarchy works will depend on the structure of your organization but this figure serves as an example

Planning to support objectives takes place at different levels within organizations. As objectives are set at different organizational levels, there are plans at each level to support the achievement of the objectives. So in your organization there will be a hierarchy of objectives and plans. See Figure 1.3 for an illustration of the organizational hierarchy of objectives and plans. (See *Activities Management*, Chapter 2, for more details.)

Activity 3

What sort of planning activities are you involved in at work?

See Feedback section for answer to this activity.

Investigate 1

Find out what you can about the objectives of your organization and department. How are you performing against your objectives? How is organizational and team performance measured?

Types of plans

Strategic plans

Strategic planning is long-term planning carried out by senior managers. The time scale for this type of planning can be up to five years.

Operational plans

Operational planning is medium-term planning carried out by middle managers and departmental managers. The time scale is usually one year. (See *Activities Management*, Chapter 2, for more details.)

Action plans

Action plans are the level of planning in which the team leader is most intimately involved. Action plans are about getting things done at work on a day-by-day, week-by-week, basis. Action planning tends to be short-term planning carried out by first line managers and supervisors.

We will concentrate on looking at action planning, which is a vital part of a team leader's role. An action plan is a step-by-step approach detailing the breakdown of tasks to achieve a specific objective. By using an action plan in your role as a team leader you will be able to organize and plan your work schedule, enabling you to set targets and agree goals with your team. If you want to achieve your objectives, it is important to set aside time to plan. See Figure 1.4 for a sample action plan. (See *Activities Management*, Chapter 2, for more details.)

Objective	Actions (specific tasks that need to be done to achieve overall objective)	By when	By whom	Notes on progress

Figure 1.4 Action plan

Personal plans

Personal plans are often the product of an appraisal interview but can be much less formal. These are your own plans (and the plans of your colleagues) showing how you will achieve your objectives.

Investigate 2 Discover all that you can about the planning process in your organization. What are your personal objectives and plans? Were these agreed at your last appraisal interview?

Project plans

These are one-off plans which relate to a specific project. For example manufacturing a new product or introducing a new quality system.

Financial plans – budgets

A budget is a financial plan which is prepared in advance. Initially budgets are prepared for the entire organization and then, as with objectives and plans, they filter down the organization so that every department has its own budget for the financial year.

A budget expresses in financial terms the performance to be achieved during the period. In other words, it is the financial aspect of the overall plan. It will detail planned income and expenditure for the period.

A budget enables managers to have clear and specific targets for the generation of income and control of costs. A budgetary control system reports the state of the budgets on a regular basis, so that managers can continually check performance against targets and pick up any problem areas such as overspending or lack of income generation in a certain area of the business.

The planning cycle

All plans have to be carefully constructed if they are going to achieve their objectives. We will now look at a model that can be used to aid the planning process. Figure 1.5 shows the planning cycle.

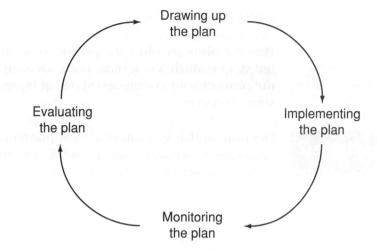

Figure 1.5
The planning cycle

Investigate 3

In what ways do you think that the managers in your organization plan for future events? How are these plans communicated to the staff? (See *Activities Management*, Chapter 2, for more details.)

The benefits of planning

There are many benefits of using systematic planning in your work:

- everyone in the team has a sense of purpose
- the working team is utilized effectively
- resources are used effectively
- planning produces better results.

(See *Activities Management*, Chapter 2, for more details.)

Organizing and coordinating

All of the activities of the team must be organized. Organizing is about making sure that all the required resources are in the right place at the right time. Organizing is about turning the plans into action. Organizing skills will be required here. It is about assigning personnel and appropriately allocating resources to accomplish a specific task. All of the activities of the team leader's work group must be organized and coordinated to ensure that everything runs smoothly and that problems are dealt with as they arise.

Organizing is ensuring that the people, instructions, equipment, materials and finance are available to complete the plan. An important part of organizing is communicating to all the people involved in doing work just what is expected of them and getting their commitment to the achievement of the plan.

Organizing is primarily concerned with deciding how the work will be done. Organizing is a primary part of the work of a team leader. It involves identifying the key tasks that need to be carried out to achieve the planning objective. To organize effectively you need to:

- Decide what actions need to be taken, by when and by whom
- gather relevant information
- consult with managers, your staff, other staff
- decide on utilization of resources – staff, materials and equipment
- delegate relevant tasks
- make sure instructions are understood.

To summarize, the stages involved in organizing are:

- examine the tasks involved in the work
- communicate the plan to everyone concerned and allocate tasks to individuals
- ensure that the necessary resources are available
- get the job started
- keep the momentum going.

Coordinating is about making sure that the team is working well together and that your team is working in a coordinated way with other teams and sections of the organization.

Motivating

The best plans, organization and coordination will not achieve the best results without a motivated team. It is part of the team leader's role to ensure that their team is motivated at work. You need to ensure that members of your team are given opportunities to obtain job satisfaction whilst they are at work. This will help to develop a team which is committed to the objectives of the organization and the team. You can do this by ensuring that your team are encouraged and developed by being given responsibility and varied tasks.

Motivation is covered in detail in Chapter 9 of this book.

Communicating

Objectives and plans need to be communicated to your workteam. A good team leader needs to keep in touch with everything that is going on in the organization. You need to keep everybody informed about what is happening. A team leader needs to have excellent communication skills; you will not be surprised to know that research has shown that team leaders spend up to 70 per cent of their day communicating with others. You need to be clear about what you need to achieve and ensure that you can communicate this clearly to your team. Communication is covered in more detail in the books in this series entitled *Information Management* and *Activities Management* (Chapter 2 for more details on communication plans).

Activity 4

How do you communicate with your team?

See Feedback section for answer to this activity.

Monitoring and controlling

Things rarely go according to plan, without any difficulties. It is important that the work of the team is coordinated and that you check progress against the plans. Monitoring systems need to be put in place for checking progress and control systems put in place so that if things are not going as planned, action can be taken.

After the plans are in place it is important that you consider how the situation will be monitored and controlled. Once the activity is planned, organized and set into motion, you have the final stage to perform: that of controlling what is going on. This entails seeing how things are going and comparing progress against the plan. If everything is running satisfactorily it is only necessary to continue to monitor the situation. However, if there is a variation from the plan, action must be taken to bring everything back in line or the plan needs to be adjusted to reflect the changed situation.

You will need to monitor progress by:

- keeping the plan in front of you
- measuring actual progress
- comparing actual progress against planned progress

THE JOB OF A TEAM LEADER

- taking corrective action if there are any variances
- making adjustments to the original plan if necessary.

When the plan is completed, always take a few moments to reflect on the overall success, or otherwise, of the plan. Be prepared to learn from any mistakes and anything that went well to improve your planning skills. (See *Activities Management*, Chapter 3 for more details.)

Activity 5	Describe how you monitor and control progress against plans at work. See Feedback section for answer to this activity.

Evaluating

A good team leader always evaluates performance and assesses the results. Evaluation is part of the control process. It is, however, important to carry out formal evaluations at regular intervals to check the performance of the team, the individuals that make up the team and the performance in relation to the task.

Activity 6	How do you evaluate the performance of your team, the individuals in the team and the team's performance in relation to the task? If you find this question difficult to answer, perhaps you need to consider what systems you need to put in place to evaluate performance in these three areas.

The importance of managing people and yourself

Management has been described by a famous American management writer, F. W. Taylor, who said that 'Management is getting things done through people'. You are only going to be able to carry out your role as a team leader if you are able to manage your team and yourself effectively. The work of a manager is about achieving the objectives by planning and organizing other people, rather than by doing the work yourself. This book concentrates on looking at how you can best manage your team and yourself to enable you to achieve your team objectives and your personal objectives. If you cannot manage your team and/or yourself, you will never be an effective team leader.

Summary

If you are a team leader you will already know that the job is complex and demanding. This chapter has covered briefly the key managerial functions carried out by a team leader. Dealing with people and managing yourself effectively will enable you to carry out your job professionally.

Review and discussion questions

1 Why do plans need to be flexible?
2 What are budgets and what are their uses?
3 List the stages of the planning cycle.
4 What are the qualities of good objectives?
5 What do you need to do, when organizing, to turn plans into actions?
6 What headings could you use to construct an action plan?
7 Why is it important to monitor and control the progress of plans?
8 What are the benefits of planning?
9 Why is it important to evaluate performance?
10 'Things happen too quickly in our job for us to do any effective planning.' Discuss this statement.

Case study

Paula is a team leader of another section of your organization. She is always overworked, she starts work early and finishes late. Her team do not appear to be overworked, they always seem to be bothering her with the type of problems that your team deal with themselves, without reference to you. She seems to just succeed in avoiding disasters. She can solve problems and handle a crisis well – she has to, because they are usually her fault. She rarely looks beyond tomorrow, and indeed she rarely has time to do so because she is handling the difficult situations that her lack of foresight causes.

Paula mentions in conversation that the job is getting on top of her. She says that she just seems to lurch from crisis to crisis. 'You've been doing this job for longer than me and you always seem to be so efficient,' says Paula. She asks for your advice. What advice would you give her to improve her performance at work?

Select a task at work that you need to plan. Complete a detailed action plan using the format below.

Objective	Actions (specific tasks that need to be done to achieve overall objective)	By when	By whom	Notes on progress

Monitor progress regularly. When the task is complete, write a brief commentary on the task which reflects on how well the plan worked and what you have learnt from the exercise. You can use headings given below.

1 The objective
2 Drawing up the plan
3 Implementing the plan
4 Monitoring the plan
5 Evaluating the plan – what I have learnt.

2 Team leaders and organizations

Learning objectives

On completion of this chapter you will be able to:

- define the term 'organization'
- differentiate between objectives and targets
- list and describe the various types of organization structure
- understand the uses and limitations of organization charts
- differentiate between tall and flat organizations
- describe the term 'culture'
- differentiate between the formal and informal culture
- explain the types of culture described by Handy and Deal and Kennedy
- appreciate the complex nature of organizational roles
- identify contributing factors to role conflict
- understand what can be done to avoid role conflict and role stress.

Introduction

In Chapter 1 we considered the job of a team leader. In this chapter we will examine the organizations in which team leaders work. The goal of all organizations is to accomplish some purpose that individuals working on their own cannot achieve. There is no widely accepted definition of the word 'organization', in fact the word can be used in two ways. Firstly to describe the planning and coordination of activities and, secondly, to describe the entity formed by a group of people. For the purposes of this chapter, we are concerned with the latter meaning of the word 'organization'. It is important that you, as a team leader working in an organization, understand the objectives of your organization. You also need to understand how your organization is structured to achieve the organization's objectives. Organizations are made up of the people who work for them; the way in which organizations work and behave cannot be explained just by analysing organizational structure, it is a little more complicated than that!

09
50
47
30
q3

In this chapter we also examine the concept of organizational culture. Organizational culture is about 'the way we do things around here'; it explains differences between organizations and why the people who work in different organizations do things in different ways and see things differently. Finally in this chapter, we look at roles that we have within organizations and some of the difficulties that are encountered in relation to job roles, we also cover the multiple roles that managers carry out in organizations.

Why we have organizations

Activity 7

Jot down your thoughts on why we have organizations.

Organizations exist for a wide variety of purposes. They all have some function to perform. They exist to achieve objectives and provide satisfaction for their members. There is a wide variety of organizations and they are all different. Examples of different types of organizations you may have been in contact with today are: school, shop, hotel, bank, bus company.

An organization could be described as 'a group of roles arranged in a structure to pursue a set of objectives.' The roles are the job roles that people have within an organization, such as Manager, Operative or Team leader. The structure is the way in which the organization is designed, i.e. how all the roles fit together in the organization. The objectives are the reasons that the organization exists, the things that the organization has been formed to achieve. This will be stated in the organization's mission statement.

Organizations are structured in a variety of different ways. The structure of the organization creates a framework within which the activities of the organization can be managed to achieve organizational objectives. In small organizations the structure is usually quite simple but in large organizations structures can be very complex. It is important that an organization is structured in the correct way so that the activities of the organization can be planned, organized, directed and controlled. The right structure will ensure that:

- resources are used effectively
- the activities of the organization are monitored and controlled
- people are accountable
- the work of the organization is coordinated
- people have a sense of belonging and the satisfaction of working in teams.

A good organization structure that supports the business objectives will assist the organization in maximizing its performance. A badly designed organization results in low morale as staff are uncertain about reporting lines and uncertain about where decisions are made. There is often insufficient delegation, conflict, lack of coordination and the organization is slow to respond to changes in the environment. Poor structures are inefficient and wasteful of resources.

Organizational objectives

We know already that organizations are formed to enable the achievement of objectives; we have looked at objectives in relation to the work of a team leader in Chapter 1. We will now look at organizational objectives in a little more detail.

What is an objective?

An objective is an end result, goal or target that an organization, department or an individual seeks to reach. Organizational objectives flow from the organization's mission or vision statement. British Aerospace's vision statement is shown in Figure 2.1.

Figure 2.1
British Aerospace's vision statement

> At British Aerospace we are dedicated to working together, and with our partners, to become The Benchmark for our industry, setting the standard for customer satisfaction, technology, financial performance and quality in all that we do.

What is your organization's vision or mission statement?

Areas for which objectives are set

You can see that a mission statement is very general and so, if the overall mission is going to be achieved, more specific objectives are required in order that the senior managers can see more clearly what needs to be done to achieve the overall aim set out in the mission statement. Objectives at this next level are often called strategic objectives or corporate objectives. A writer, Peter Drucker has suggested that organizational objectives should be set in the following areas:

1 market standing
2 productivity
3 physical and financial resources
4 profitability
5 innovation
6 manager performance and development
7 worker performance and attitudes
8 public and social responsibility.

Investigate 5

Get a copy of the corporate objectives of your organization. Do they cover the eight areas that Drucker suggested organizational objectives should cover?

Once the strategic/corporate objectives have been decided upon, objectives are set for each department in the organization. Within each department, each team will have objectives and so every area and level within the organization has a set of objectives to achieve. If all the objectives throughout the organization are achieved, the organization will achieve its overall aims and so fulfil its mission statement.

Increasingly the payment of staff, particularly managers, is linked in some way to performance against the objectives, i.e. performance-related pay.

Do you have performance-related pay in your organization? Is payment under this system related to the achievement of objectives?

Targets

As objectives work their way down the organization they become much more specific; very specific objectives are known as targets. If you are currently a team leader you may have targets set which your team needs to achieve and the achievement of those targets may form the basis for some of the discussion at your annual appraisal interview.

If you and your colleagues are to achieve your objectives and targets they must be soundly conceived. In Chapter 1 we established that good objectives are **SMART**; so are good targets. In addition, objectives and targets should be worthwhile and inspiring, they should be visible, they should be communicated to the people who need to achieve them and should be linked to the higher objectives of the organization.

The team leader's role when dealing with objectives and targets is to clarify them for the team, communicate them to the team and make sure that the team members know what they must do. It is also important to continually monitor performance against targets and to let the team know how they are doing.

If an organization does not have targets it, and the people who comprise it, lack a sense of direction, initiative is not encouraged, effort can be badly aimed, opportunities are missed to motivate staff by recognizing achievement and, at worst, there may be no improvement, or even a decline, in overall performance.

Types of organization structure

There are various ways in which organizations are structured. Large organizations may display different structures at different levels within the organization. Some of the most common structures are described below.

Functional

In a functional structure, the common functions or similar activities are grouped together to form a unit within the organization, such as marketing, accounting, personnel, production and so on. Functional departmentalization may occur at any level within the organization and it is often found near the top. A typical chart of a functional organization is shown in Figure 2.2.

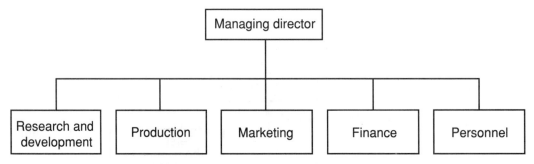

Figure 2.2 A typical functional organization. Reprinted by permission of Bankers Books. From *Supervisory Skills* by Sally Palmer (1996).

Product

Some organizations group activities on the basis of product. This is particularly popular in organizations that produce a wide range of products or provide a wide range of services. An example of a chart illustrating a product-based structure is shown in Figure 2.3.

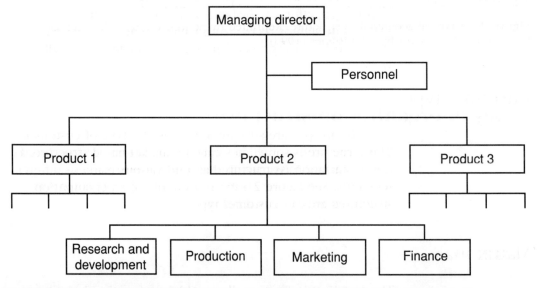

Figure 2.3 Example of a product-based structure. Reprinted by permission of Bankers Books. From *Supervisory Skills* by Sally Palmer (1996).

PEOPLE AND SELF MANAGEMENT

21

Geographical

As businesses expand, an organization structure is often designed around the geography of the business. This structure is often adopted in a large business where there is a national or international network of branches. A typical structure is shown in Figure 2.4.

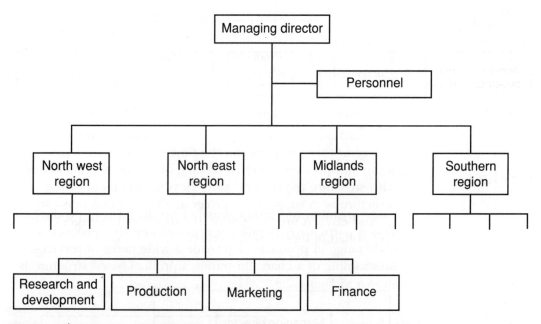

Figure 2.4 A typical geographical structure. Reprinted by permission of Bankers Books. From *Supervisory Skills* by Sally Palmer (1996).

Customer type

Some businesses are structured around the type of customer. This structure is sometimes called a market-based structure, as the organization is structured around various market segments. See Figure 2.5 for an example of an organization structured around customer type.

Matrix

The matrix structure usually combines a functional structure with a project-based structure. A chart illustrating a matrix

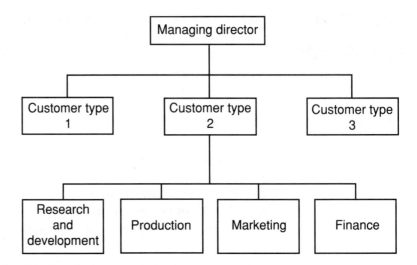

Figure 2.5
Example of a
customer-type
structure. Reprinted
by permission of
Bankers Books. From
Supervisory Skills by
Sally Palmer (1996).

structure is shown in Figure 2.6. The project managers are in
charge of their projects and the functional managers have
input and provide a service to each of the project managers.
This structure tends to be more flexible; the focus of the
structure is to support the projects, although conflicts can
occur between project groups and functional managers can
feel pulled in too many directions.

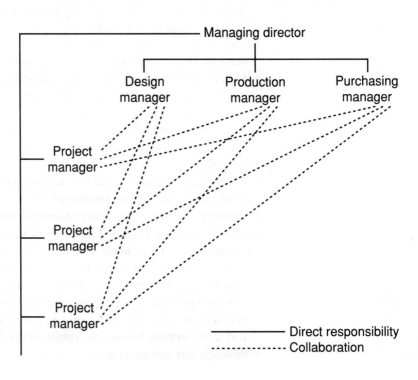

Figure 2.6
Example of a matrix
structure. Reprinted
by permission of
Bankers Books. From
Supervisory Skills by
Sally Palmer (1996).

PEOPLE AND SELF MANAGEMENT

| Activity 8 | Draw an organization chart of your own **organization**. How would you describe the structure? |

Organization charts

The structure of an organization is usually illustrated in the form of an organization chart. The chart shows the reader a picture of the organization. Organization charts can be very useful and can be used as a management tool to indicate weaknesses and to review the organizational structure. They can be used as a guide for staff and outsiders, a map to explain the organization to newcomers, a means of identifying undefined responsibilities or overlaps. A chart could assist in locating the person to report to, re-allocating duties, to help to sort out demarcation disputes, to aid the process of job evaluation. An organization chart shows several key aspects of the organization, as shown below:

- *Division of labour* – an organization chart illustrates how human resources are organized to benefit from the division of labour which allows people to specialize and concentrate on doing jobs for which they have been specifically trained or have specific expertise.
- *Chain of command* – the chart depicts the formal authority responsibility relationships throughout the organization.
- *Unity of command* – the chart illustrates whether there is unity of command, i.e. whether each individual is accountable to only one person.
- *Departmentalization* – an organization chart illustrates how the organization has grouped its activities to best achieve its objectives.
- *Levels of hierarchy* – the chart demonstrates how many levels there are in the hierarchy.
- *Span of control* – the span of control refers to the number of subordinates responsible to each superior so, for example, if a team leader has five team members, the span of control is five. A narrow span of control allows for close supervision, better communication and reduced delegation. A wide span of control gives subordinates greater decision-making authority, means lower management costs and less control, but it can result in greater motivation through job satisfaction.

Activity 9

Now draw an organization chart of your **department**. Ensure that the chart clearly demonstrates all the features described on page 23.

Tall organizations and flat organizations

The span of control determines the 'shape' of the organization. A tall organization has a long management hierarchy with many layers of management between the lowest and the highest level in the organization, spans of control tend to be smaller in a tall organization. Figure 2.7 depicts a tall organization.

Chief Executive
|
Divisional Directors
|
Departmental Managers
|
Section Heads
|
Group Team Leaders
|
Team Leaders
|
Assistant Team Leaders
|
Operatives

Figure 2.7
A tall organization.
Reprinted by
permission of Bankers
Books. From
Supervisory Skills by
Sally Palmer (1996).

A flat organization, as shown in Figure 2.8, is one in which there are wider spans of control and fewer levels in the hierarchy. Over recent years, many organizations have tended to 'de-layer', that is, remove layers of management from the hierarchy resulting in flatter organizations and wider spans of control.

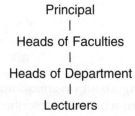

Principal
|
Heads of Faculties
|
Heads of Department
|
Lecturers

Figure 2.8
A flat organization

PEOPLE AND SELF MANAGEMENT

| Activity 10 | Look at the organization charts that you drew in Activities 8 and 9 above. Is your organization flat or tall? |

The limitations of organization charts

Organization charts do have limitations, however. The organization chart does not show how informal groups operate within the formal organizational structure. They do not show the extent of delegation and it is sometimes difficult to show lateral/horizontal communication across the organization. They also become out of date very quickly.

Organizational culture

Another important aspect of an organization is organizational culture. The culture of an organization is something that develops and changes over a period of time. Culture is often described as 'the way we do things around here'. It is about the organization's past achievements, present mission and objectives, attitudes to staff, customers and suppliers. Every organization has its own unique culture. Culture helps to explain differences between organizations and it helps to explain why different organizations and the people who work in the organizations see things differently. There are two types of culture:

- *The formal culture* - the formal culture is represented by the company's annual report, the organizational mission, organizational beliefs and organizational objectives. The formal organizational culture creates the way in which the organization behaves and organizational attitudes to customers, staff and suppliers.
- *The informal culture* - the way in which the culture operates may be different from the official definitions. The informal culture is about the beliefs and behaviour of the staff in the organization; the informal culture is based on the reality.

Handy on culture

Charles Handy wrote about organizational culture. He defined four types of culture which are described in Figure 2.9.

Type of culture	Diagrammatic representation of the culture	Description of the culture
Power	Depicted as a web	Centralization of power is a key feature of this culture. Frequently found in small organizations where power rests with an individual or a small group of individuals. **Advantages** Decisions made quickly by a few powerful individuals. **Disadvantages** Individuals suppressed by a few powerful people. Individuals not motivated because there is a lack of challenge. If the organization gets too big the web will break.
Role	Depicted as a Greek temple	Typically a bureaucratic organization. Hierarchical, officers and officials. Functional structure. Job descriptions, rules and procedures. Power is hierarchical and determined by position. **Advantages** Rules and procedures are the main source of influence and job descriptions ensure that people carry out their jobs. **Disadvantages** Little scope for initiative and individual growth and development.
Task	Depicted as a net	Project orientated. A team culture with an emphasis on the task. The task determines the way in which the work is organized. **Advantages** Employees have considerable freedom. Flexibility makes task cultures rewarding to work in. **Disadvantages** Lack of 'formal' authority can make task cultures difficult to manage.
Person	Depicted as a cluster – a galaxy of individual stars	The organization exists to serve the needs of the individuals in it. Individuals are central. Not often found in profit-motivated enterprises. No hierarchies. **Advantages** Highly satisfying to some individuals **Disadvantages** Difficult to remain as an organization

Figure 2.9 Culture according to Handy

Deal and Kennedy on culture

Deal and Kennedy studied hundreds of organizations and categorized culture in a different way. They found four types of culture in the organizations they studied: the tough-guy macho culture, the work-hard/play-hard culture, the bet-your-company culture, the process culture.

- *Tough-guy macho culture – 'find a mountain and climb it'*. An organization of individuals. High risk, high financial stakes, focus on speed. Intense pressure. Internal competition. Examples: police departments, surgeons, construction, cosmetics, management consulting and the entertainment industry.
- *Work-hard/play-hard culture – 'find a need and fill it'*. Fun and action. Few risks. Dynamic organizations focusing on customers and their needs. Examples: estate agents, computer companies and retail stores.
- *Bet-your-company culture – 'slow and steady wins the race'*. Large-stake, high-risk decisions. Hierarchical decisions made from the top down. Examples: oil companies, investment banks, architectural firms and the forces. A slow-moving culture.
- *Process culture – 'it's not what you do it's the way that you do it'*. A low-risk culture. Employees find it difficult to measure what they do. Reports and memos seem to disappear. Lack of feedback forces employees to concentrate on how they do something, not what they do. Attention to trivial events, minor detail and technical perfection. Examples: banks, insurance companies, financial services and the civil service.

Activity 11

Think about your own organization, compare it with the classifications of organizational culture described by Handy and Deal and Kennedy. How would you describe the culture of your organization?

Roles

We have already defined an organization as 'a group of roles arranged in a structure to pursue a set of objectives'. We have examined the terms 'objectives' and 'structure' mentioned in the above definition. We will now examine the term 'role'.

In an organizational sense roles are the jobs that people do within the organization. The organization achieves its objectives through the 'role structure' of the organization. The term 'role' has been defined by Laurie Mullins, as 'the expected pattern of behaviours associated with members occupying a particular position within the structure of an organization'. The role that we have within an organization has a strong influence on how we behave in the workplace.

Our role determines how we dress and how we speak. We not only have roles that influence our behaviour at work, but we have a multitude of other roles in life such as child to our parents, parent of our children, partner or spouse, treasurer of the squash club, student at college. When we adopt each role that we have in our life, we behave and react in different ways.

Activity 12

List eight roles that you play in your private and working life.

See Feedback section for answer to this activity.

Activity 13

Did you change any aspect of your behaviour at work when you were promoted to the role of team leader?

If you are absolutely honest with yourself you probably did change some aspects of the way you behave at work.

New roles

When we move into a new role, for example, a new job or parenthood for the first time, we watch how others behave and adapt our behaviour to the new role. When we start a new job we have to learn how to behave in the new role.

Role set

A role set is the set of roles that a person has contact with in their job role. Examples of a team leader's role set might be, senior managers, line manager, other supervisors, the supervisor's team, customers, friends, colleagues in other teams, personnel department, the Trade Union.

PEOPLE AND SELF MANAGEMENT

Role expectations

This term describes what a person is expected to do in their role. Formal expectations relating to the role are specified by the organization, they will be set down in a job description and in a person's contract of employment. There are also informal role expectations which are imposed by the working group, such as methods of communicating, dress, supporting team members and attitudes towards senior managers.

Role conflict

Role conflict occurs when a person in a role has difficulty in carrying out that role for one reason or another. There are various aspects of role conflict, these are described below.

Role incompatibility

This arises when a person faces a situation in which different people have different expectations of that person and the expectations are incompatible. For example, the team that you supervise expects you to be able to arrange for them all to leave early to attend a Christmas celebration but the management expect you to ensure that all the work is finished before anyone leaves work.

Role ambiguity

This occurs when it is not made clear exactly what a person's job role is. The person in the role is then not sure exactly what is expected of them. This often occurs when a new job is created and a satisfactory job description has not been drawn up.

Role overload

If a person has too many roles to handle in their job they may suffer from role overload. For example, if a person, in addition to their normal job role as a team leader, is leading a quality improvement team, is the Union representative for the office and the safety representative for the office, there could be a conflict of priority. Role conflict could result as the person attempts to prioritize and juggle all their roles. (Role overload must not be confused with work overload, which is when a person has too much work to do.)

Role underload

This occurs when the role which needs fulfilling to meet the objectives of the organization is held by a person who believes that the role is not sufficiently demanding to satisfy them. The person may feel that they are not stretched enough and could do a more demanding job.

Role stress

All of the situations described and explained above under role conflict can lead to role stress. If a person suffers from role stress their performance will decline and they will not be satisfied in their work.

Avoiding role conflict and role stress

It is important for organizations to have systems in place to avoid problems with role conflict and role stress. This can be done by ensuring that:

- there are detailed job descriptions in place
- the organization's recruitment and selection procedures match the right people to the right jobs
- people are properly trained and prepared for the role that they are expected to undertake
- managers and supervisors are trained to spot stress-related problems
- staff clearly understand what is expected of them.

PEOPLE AND SELF MANAGEMENT

Investigate 7

Think carefully about the above ways of avoiding role conflict. Does your organization ensure that everything possible is done to avoid role conflict?

Managerial roles

Henry Mintzberg made a study of how executives spent their time whilst they were at work. His research was based on senior managers within an organization, but it is just as important that you understand the various roles that your managers undertake, as well as understanding the various roles that you carry out. A good team leader needs to view their role in the context of the roles of everyone in the organization. Mintzberg identified ten different managerial roles which he classified into three areas. These are explained in Figure 2.10.

INTERPERSONAL ROLES	These roles arise from the manager's position and status in the organization and are related to relations with other people.
Figurehead	Being available for people who want to speak to the person 'in charge' or 'at the top', entertaining visitors, attending social events, making speeches. Activities where the manager is the symbol of the organization.
Leader	A very important role, motivating and guiding staff and maintaining morale.
Liaison	Relationships with individuals and groups outside the department or organization, establishing and being in networks outside the group for the benefit of the group

INFORMATIONAL ROLES	These roles are about the communication and information aspects of a manager's job.
Monitor	Gathering information, from inside and outside the organization and using it to monitor the environment.
Disseminator	Passing external information into the organization, and clarifying and interpreting that information.
Spokesperson	The manager as an expert on group activities dealing with people outside the group.

DECISIONAL ROLES	This set of roles relates to decision making and access to information. They are based on the manager's status and authority.
Entrepreneur	Initiating business projects, bringing about change by seeking and exploiting new opportunities for the group.
Disturbance handler	Monitoring and handling unusual situations and unpredicted events which disturb the normal work.
Resource allocator	The manager ensures the effective allocation and use of organizational resources to achieve organizational objectives.
Negotiator	Negotiating both inside and outside the organization and representing and obtaining the best possible deal for the group in these negotiations.

Figure 2.10 Mintzberg's managerial roles. Reprinted by permission of Bankers Books. From *Supervisory Skills* by Sally Palmer (1996).

Activity 14

Consider the job of a manager in your organization. Think about each one of the managerial roles described by Mintzberg and complete the table below.

INTERPERSONAL ROLES	Example of an activity carried out by a manager in my organization that fulfills this role
Figurehead	
Leader	
Liaison	

INFORMATIONAL ROLES	Example of an activity carried out by a manager in my organization that fulfills this role
Monitor	
Disseminator	
Spokesperson	

DECISIONAL ROLES	Example of an activity carried out by a manager in my organization that fulfills this role
Entrepreneur	
Disturbance handler	
Resource allocator	
Negotiator	

Summary

In this chapter we have looked at why we have organizations and the importance of organizational objectives, organizational structure and culture. An understanding of the type of organization in which you work will help you to understand your role in the organization.

We have looked at the role of the team leader within the organization. We know that the role is demanding and complex – you will definitely already know this if you are a team leader! Team leaders are generally being given more and more responsibility as organizations become flatter, there are fewer layers of management and decision-making is being pushed further down the organization. You need drive and energy, good management skills and the knowledge required to do the job. You have a responsibility for the well-being of your team, for delivering products or services on time and of a high quality and you are part of the management team. This book and all the books in the Team Leader Series will help you to improve all aspects of your management skills and become more effective in your increasingly demanding first line management role. For those of you who are not yet a team leader, this text will provide you with an excellent grounding to help you face the challenges of being in your first management role.

Review and discussion questions

1 Define the term 'organization'.
2 What is a mission statement?
3 What do you understand by the term 'hierarchy of objectives'?
4 What is the difference between objectives and targets?
5 Describe the supervisor's role in dealing with objectives and targets.
6 What are the uses of organization charts?
7 Explain the term 'span of control'.
8 Differentiate between a tall and a flat organization.
9 In an organizational sense, what are roles?
10 Explain the term 'role set'.
11 What is meant by 'role expectations'?
12 List four problems with roles that can lead to role stress.
13 List the three areas into which Mintzberg classified manager's roles.
14 What phrase is often used to describe culture?
15 Briefly describe the four cultures identified by Handy.

TEAM LEADERS AND ORGANIZATIONS

Case study

Things had been going well for Abdul. His wife had just had their first child, which he was delighted about. It did mean, though, that he was not getting much sleep and found it difficult to stay late at work on the odd occasion when a problem flared up, as he had to get home to help out there.

Also, Abdul was recently promoted to the position of team leader. It was a well deserved promotion: he was a hard worker who showed great potential, he was generally considered to be fair and was well liked by everybody. He said when he first took the job, 'I'm not going to change just because I'm a team leader now, I've always been one of the lads, that's the way I am'. When he first became a team leader his team were delighted as they all liked Abdul. However, Abdul has started to experience a few problems in his team. One or two people have been arriving for work a little late in the morning and taking extended coffee breaks; the general consensus of opinion seems to be that Abdul would not mind, he is a good bloke. Abdul has tried speaking to the people who are causing the problems but they do not seem to be taking him seriously.

On top of this problem he is finding being a first-time father quite demanding, especially since his wife returned to work full time. Abdul is now beginning to wonder if he did the right thing in accepting the job; he likes the work and most of the team are working well but he does seem to have problems getting some of the team to take him seriously. With this, and the pressures at home, he feels that everything is getting on top of him.

Abdul asks for your advice. How do you explain the reasons for the pressures that Abdul feels to him? What can you suggest that Abdul does to tackle his problems?

Work-based assignment

C12.1

1 Describe the way your organization is structured, then explain the reasons for the structure and comment on its effectiveness.

2 What are organizational objectives and what should their purpose be? Comment on the way in which your organizational objectives are conveyed to you and to the staff in your team. Give your opinion, with reasons, on whether they have any practical effect on how you work.

3 Workteams

Learning objectives

On completion of this chapter you will be able to:

- differentiate between groups and teams
- explain the importance of the Hawthorne Experiments
- explain the stages of team development
- recognize the importance of team norms and team boundaries
- describe the term 'team cohesiveness' and appreciate the factors that contribute to a cohesive team
- differentiate between effective and ineffective workteams
- describe Belbin's nine management team roles.

Introduction

Work is a group activity and if an organization is to function effectively it requires teams of people to work well together. Teams are formed by the organization in order to get jobs done most effectively. In the work situation most tasks are undertaken by teams, rather than by individuals. Team leaders manage teams of people at work and ensure that the team they lead achieves the objectives it needs to in order that the organization achieves its overall objectives. Obviously, it is important for you to understand a great deal about the way teams behave at work.

Groups and teams

A group is more than an aimless crowd of people waiting for a train or standing in a queue in a shop. A group is a collection of individuals, with a central purpose, under the

direction of a leader and who share a sense of common
identity. A group is:

> *any number of people who*
>
> * *interact with one another;*
> * *are psychologically aware of one another; and*
> * *perceive themselves to be a group.*

A team is more than a group. Effective teams consist of
people who can:

* work together
* are loyal to each other
* feel committed and are motivated to achieve a high level of
  output
* care how other members of the team feel
* are open with each other and listen to each other
* have common goals
* are prepared to work conflict through.

Collaboration, i.e. working together is the keynote of team
activity. Effective teams have clear objectives and agreed goals;
they are open and do not avoid confrontation; the members
support and trust one another. The members all work together
in an atmosphere of cooperation; conflicts are open and
resolved by the team; there are sound procedures in place and
good leadership. The team regularly reviews its own
performance and individuals are encouraged to develop within
the team.

The importance of belonging to a team at work

It is very important to individuals to feel that they are a
member of a team at work. A famous management writer,
Elton Mayo, carried out a series of experiments in the late
1920s to early 1930s which demonstrated how important it
was to people at work to be a member of a workteam. These
experiments became very famous and are known as The
Hawthorne Experiments. See Figure 3.1 for a description of
the experiments.

At the time the results generated new ideas about the
importance of work groups, leadership, communications,

From 1924 to 1932 a series of studies was carried out at the Hawthorne plant of the Western Electric Company in the USA. The Hawthorne Experiments helped to bring in a new emphasis on human relations. There were four main phases to the Hawthorne Experiments:

1 The illumination experiments

Initially the studies were concerned with testing scientific principles. The first experiment was concerned with measuring the effect on output of different levels of lighting. For this the experimenters worked with two small samples of female employees, an experimental group and a control group. However, a surprise result was that a reduction in lighting did not lead to a fall in output – in fact output increased up to the point at which it was virtually too dark to see.

What had happened? It was clear that the level of production was influenced by factors other than the physical conditions at work. These results prompted a series of further tests.

To the surprise of the researchers, it was the taking an interest in what workers were doing that had raised their motivation, interest and efforts. No longer were the women isolated individuals, working together only in the sense of being near each other. They had become participating members of a working group with all the psychological and social implications peculiar to such a group. Since that time the 'Hawthorne effect' has been used to describe the situation in which an experimenter's interest in people being studied induces those people to work harder.

2 The relay assembly room

The work in the relay assembly room was repetitive and boring. The researchers selected six people and subjected them to a series of changes to their conditions of work, such as hours of work, rest pauses and provision of refreshments. The observers conducting the experiments adopted a friendly manner to the workers, consulting with them and listening to any problems that occurred. Following all but one of the changes there was a continuous increase in the level of production. The researchers concluded that it was the extra attention given to the workers that was the main reason for the higher productivity.

3 The interviewing programme

In an attempt to find out more about the workers' feelings towards their supervisors and conditions of work, an interviewing programme was introduced. More than 20 000 interviews were conducted. The interviewers adopted a friendly approach to the interviewees. They found out a great deal about the workers' true feelings and attitudes towards, not just supervision and working conditions, but to the company, management and group relations. The interviewing programme was significant as it highlighted the need to listen to the workers' feelings and problems.

4 The bank wiring observation room

This experiment involved the observation of 14 men working in the bank wiring room. The researchers noticed that the men formed their own informal organization with sub-groups or cliques and that natural leaders emerged. There was a financial incentive scheme so that the workers could earn more money, the more work that they produced. Despite this scheme the men limited output to well below the level they were capable of producing. This was because the group believed that if their output was too high, management would raise their expectations about what workers could produce whilst they were working. The group pressures on every member of the group from the rest of the group were stronger than the offer of financial bonuses.

Figure 3.1 The Hawthorne Experiments

WORKTEAMS

motivation and job design. The main conclusions from the experiments were that:

- work is a group activity, individual workers cannot be seen in isolation
- workers have a need for recognition, security and a sense of belonging which is more important than financial incentives and physical conditions at work
- informal groups exercise a strong social control over work habits and the attitudes of the individual worker
- team leaders and managers need to be aware of these social needs and cater for them if workers are to collaborate with the official organization rather than work against it.

The conclusions of the Hawthorne Experiments have some very important messages for team leaders today. The experiments demonstrate how important it is to build team spirit and to recognize and value the work of your team. They also underline how important it is to ensure that informal groups and the formal team at work are working towards the same objectives.

Team formation and development

Teams take time to develop into a productive, efficient working team. A writer, Tuckman, has studied the development of teams. He said that teams move through four stages of development: forming, storming, norming and performing, as illustrated in Figure 3.2.

If you are aware of these stages, it will help you to understand the behaviour of your team and the teams that you come into contact with who are passing through the various stages of team development.

Team norms

At stage three of Tuckman's model, team norms develop. The importance of norms was first discovered in the Hawthorne Experiments. Norms are standards of social and work behaviour that are expected of individuals within the team by the rest of the team. Once norms have developed, there are strong pressures from other members of the team to conform to them.

PEOPLE AND SELF MANAGEMENT

Stage 1, forming	The initial forma • finding their • finding out • finding way • anxious • acquiring • relying or • getting t • learning
Stage 2, storming	Member may be: • internal conflict • conflict between factions within the team • flaring up of emotions • challenges to the position of the leader • an emotional reaction against the task
Stage 3, norming	Conflict is settled, the team members are: • cooperating with one another • exchanging views • setting new standards and norms • becoming cohesive • supporting each other
Stage 4, performing	The group has progressed successfully through its stages of development, real progress is made, and: • teamwork is achieved • roles are flexible • solutions are found and implemented • team energy is directed towards completion of the task • constructive work forges ahead

Figure 3.2 Stages of team development

...times team norms and organizational norms are in ...ict with one another, as in the Hawthorne Experiments ...en the workers restricted output. Typical team norms are ...ot to produce at too high a rate, not to shirk, not to say anything to team leaders or managers which might harm members of the team, not to be officious where, for example, a member of the team has responsibility for quality control. If team members do not conform to norms teams develop their own *sanctions*, for example, sending a member of the team 'to Coventry', being sarcastic to them, not passing on information to them or even expelling them from the team or trying to damage their career.

The ideal situation for the organization is when the team norms and the organizational norms are in harmony with one another. It is important for you, as a team leader, to secure this harmony in your own section.

Activity 15

List five of the work norms in your workteam.

Team boundaries

Teams have boundaries around them that define who is, and who is not, in the team. Teams will only allow certain people to enter. Those within the team display the norms for that team and anybody entering the team has to conform to those norms to be accepted. People can be in several teams and when in a particular team display the norms of that team. When a new member joins the team, if they are welcome, the other team members or one member of the team will ease them into the team and explain the expected behaviours, i.e. the norms of the team.

Team cohesiveness

Team cohesiveness refers to the ability of team members to stick together and the ability of the team to attract new members. A very cohesive team demonstrates a strong loyalty to individual members and a strong adherence to its established norms. Individuals who cannot accept the team norms are cast out from the protection of the team. Cohesive teams do not necessarily produce a higher level of output, as demonstrated by the Hawthorne Experiments, but cohesive teams usually result in greater interaction between members, mutual help and social satisfaction. There are several factors which contribute to team cohesiveness. These are shown in Figure 3.3.

Similarity of work	Where the nature of the task is similar cohesiveness is usually greater
Physical setting	Where workers are close together cohesiveness is generally increased
Communications	Where members can communicate freely with each other there is a greater likelihood of team cohesiveness
Permanence of group members	Team relationships take time to develop. Frequent changes of membership tend to lead to a less cohesive team
Group size	Cohesiveness becomes more difficult to achieve when the team is too large
External threat	Cohesiveness is often enhanced by members cooperating with one another when faced with a common external threat
Success	The more successful the team, the more cohesive it is likely to be
Leadership style of the manager	The form of management and style of leadership will affect team cohesiveness. Where the leader is supportive and participative, cohesiveness will increase
Common social factors (age, race, social status etc.)	The more similar background, interests, attitudes and values are, the more cohesive the team tends to be

Figure 3.3
Factors contributing
to cohesive teams

Activity 16

How cohesive is your team? Complete the table below.

Factor influencing cohesiveness	Comment in relation to my team
Similarity of work	
Physical setting	
Communications	
Permanence of group members	
Group size	
External threat	
Success	
My leadership style	
Common social factors (age, race, social status etc.)	

Effective and ineffective teams

Douglas McGregor, provided an account of the differences between effective and ineffective work groups. These are summarized in Figure 3.4.

Effective teams	Ineffective teams
1 Informal, relaxed atmosphere	Bored or tense atmosphere
2 Much relevant discussion with a high degree of participation	Discussion dominated by one or two people and often irrelevant
3 Team objective understood and commitment to it obtained	No clear common objective
4 Members listen to each other	Members tend not to listen to each other
5 Conflict is not avoided but brought out into the open and dealt with constructively	Conflict is either avoided or allowed to develop into open warfare
6 Most decisions are reached by general consensus	Simple majorities are seen as sufficient basis for group decisions, which the majority have to accept
7 Ideas are expressed freely and openly	Personal feelings are kept hidden and criticism is embarrassing
8 Leadership is not always with the formal leader but tends to be shared openly	Leadership is provided by the formal leader
9 The team examines its own progress and behaviour	The team avoids any discussion about its own behaviour
10 Low staff turnover and absenteeism	High staff turnover and absenteeism

Figure 3.4
Effective and
ineffective teams

Activity 17

How effective is your team? Complete the table below.

Effective teams	Ineffective teams	My comments on how effective my team is
1 Informal, relaxed atmosphere	Bored or tense atmosphere	
2 Much relevant discussion with a high degree of participation	Discussion dominated by one or two people, and often irrelevant	
3 Team objective understood, and commitment to it obtained	No clear common objective	
4 Members listen to each other	Members tend not to listen to each other	
5 Conflict is not avoided but brought out into the open and dealt with constructively	Conflict is either avoided or allowed to develop into open warfare	
6 Most decisions are reached by general consensus	Simple majorities are seen as sufficient basis for group decisions, which the majority have to accept	
7 Ideas are expressed freely and openly	Personal feelings are kept hidden and criticism is embarrassing	
8 Leadership is not always with the formal leader but tends to be shared openly	Leadership is provided by the formal leader	
9 The team examines its own progress and behaviour	The team avoids any discussion about its own behaviour	
10 Low staff turnover and absenteeism	High staff turnover and absenteeism	

Management team roles – the work of Belbin

Figure 3.5
Belbin's team roles.
Reprinted with
permission from
Belbin, R.M. (1993)
Team Roles at Work,
Butterworth-
Heinemann

A researcher from Cambridge, Meredith Belbin, has
conducted in-depth research into the membership of
successful teams. He concluded that teams composed of
similar people will not work well together and lack
creativity. Belbin identified nine team roles. An explanation
of these roles is given in Figure 3.5. Belbin states that these

Roles and descriptions – team-role contribution		Allowable weaknesses
Plant:	Creative, imaginative, unorthodox. Solves difficult problems.	Ignores details. Too preoccupied to communicate effectively.
Resource investigator:	Extrovert, enthusiastic, communicative. Explores opportunities. Develops contacts.	Overoptimistic. Loses interest once initial enthusiasm has passed.
Co-ordinator:	Mature, confident, a good chairperson. Clarifies goals, promotes decision-making. Delegates well.	Can be seen as manipulative. Delegates personal work.
Shaper:	Challenging, dynamic, thrives on pressure. Has the drive and courage to overcome obstacles.	Can provoke others. Hurts people's feelings.
Monitor-Evaluator:	Sober, strategic and discerning. Sees all options. Judges accurately.	Lacks drive and ability to inspire others. Overly critical.
Team Worker:	Co-operative, mild, perceptive and diplomatic. Listens, builds, avoids, friction, calms the waters.	Indecisive in crunch situations. Can be easily influenced.
Implementer:	Disciplined, reliable, conservative and efficient. Turns ideas into practical actions.	Somewhat inflexible. Slow to respond to new possibilities.
Completer:	Painstaking, conscientious, anxious. Searches out errors and omissions. Delivers on time.	Inclined to worry unduly. Reluctant to delegate. Can be a nit-picker
Specialist:	Single-minded, self-sharing, dedicated. Provides knowledge and skills in rare supply.	Contributes on only a narrow front. Dwells on technicalities. Overlooks the 'big picture'.

are the key team roles and that creative teams need a balance of these roles to be creative and successful. He has designed a 'Self Perception Inventory' (similar to a questionnaire) which can be completed to establish what a person's key team role is; although a person usually has a dominant role they will probably have a back-up role. Belbin claims that not all nine types are necessarily needed but a good mix of roles is important. It is an interesting exercise to conduct the Belbin Self Perception Inventory for your team. You can find out what roles people have within your team and see what team roles you are short of. If you have this information you can more easily compensate for the roles that you do not have. Some organizations use Belbin's Self Perception Inventory when putting a workteam together to ensure that all the key roles are covered.

Summary

In your job as team leader it is important for you to work to create an environment in which your team can work effectively. We will look in more detail at how you can do that in Chapter 5, 'Leading your team'. However, you now know how important it is to have clear objectives for your team, you are aware of the stages of team development and the significance of team norms and boundaries on the behaviour of your team. We have also covered the factors that contribute to creating cohesive teams and you know how to recognize effective and ineffective teams. If you have carried out all the activities in the chapter you will have analysed your team and have a good idea of any areas which need working on.

Review and discussion questions

1 Differentiate between the terms 'group' and 'team'.
2 What were the conclusions of the Hawthorne researchers?
3 List the four stages of group development.
4 List five of the factors that influence team cohesiveness.
5 How can you distinguish between effective and ineffective work groups?
6 List Belbin's nine management team roles.
7 What sort of difficulties are caused by having a 'loner' in a working group? How should a team leader respond in these circumstances?

8 You have just been introduced to Hilda, a newly recruited junior member of staff, and asked to 'look after her and get her into your group'. What problems might you anticipate, and how would you cope with them?

Case study You have just been promoted to the position of team leader. Your team has been working together for five years and has had the same team leader since the team was formed. Your predecessor has just retired and his team members are very sad to see him go. They have told you that they 'had a great working relationship with Geoff' and they do not know if anyone can replace him. Your manager has told you that there are problems with the team; output is not as good as some other teams; they do not join in with the other teams; they seem to perceive themselves as being different, special, superior to the others in some way. There is certainly no justification for them to consider themselves superior based on their current and past performance. There have been some problems with conflict between your team and other teams. How will you go about resolving the problems that you have inherited with this team?

Work-based assignment

C9.1
C9.2

Work through the following checklist and apply it to your own team. Think about each point and, ask yourself if your team needs development in this area. Compile an action plan detailing what you are going to do to improve the performance of your team.

Area of activity	My comments on the current situation	What I need to do to improve the performance of my team in this area
Learning new skills		
Tackling new tasks		
Communicating with each other		
Communicating with other teams		
Striving for high levels of output		
Striving for high quality		
Thinking up new ideas		
Finding better ways of doing things		
Setting high safety standards		
Supporting each other		
Becoming more self-sufficient		
Learning new job roles		
Sharing decision making		
Seeking new team challenges		
Evaluating team performance		

4 Recruiting and selecting your team

Learning objectives

On completion of this chapter you will be able to:

- appreciate the importance of human resource planning
- outline the stages of the recruitment and selection process
- conduct a simple job analysis
- devise a job description
- construct a personnel specification
- list appropriate sources of recruitment
- explain the key features that a job advertisement should have
- participate in a selection interview
- appreciate the importance of induction.

Introduction

The human resources – the people – who work in an organization are the most important resource that the organization has. Every organization should have a *human resource plan* which supports the business objectives. The organization's business plan will indicate what kinds of knowledge and skills employees will require and will give an indication of the numbers of staff that will be needed for the business objectives to be achieved. A human resource plan is required to ensure that sufficient staff are recruited into the organization, staff are retained by the organization, that they are used effectively, are trained in the necessary skills and that they move out of the organization when it is appropriate.

An organization is only as good as the people who work in it. It is very important that the organization has the right kind of people who can work together to achieve the organization's objectives. *Recruitment* is the process of attracting sufficient numbers of people to apply for jobs in the organization. The aim of recruitment is to ensure that your organization has the right kind of people, and that the organization's demand for human resources is met, by attracting the right type of potential employees in a cost effective and timely manner.

The process of *selection* is about selecting the most suitable people, who have been attracted by the recruitment process, to work in the organization. The aim of selection is to identify, from those coming forward from the recruitment process, the individuals most likely to meet the needs of the organization. See Figure 4.1 for an overview of the recruitment and selection process.

Figure 4.1
An overview of the recruitment and selection process

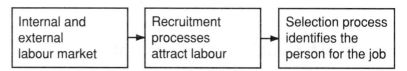

A study of this chapter will not make you an expert on human resource planning or on recruitment and selection. Human resource planning is usually carried out by senior managers. Recruitment is usually carried out by personnel specialists within the organization but the selection process is usually carried out across the organization. This chapter concentrates on dealing with the aspects of the process which you, as a first line manager, might be involved in. For example, you might be required to assist with the selection process in order to fill a job vacancy.

In this chapter we start by looking at the importance of human resource planning followed by a brief mention of the legislation that you need to be aware of if you are involved in the recruitment and selection process. The chapter then gives an overview of the recruitment and selection process before examining each aspect of the process in more detail.

Whether or not you are involved in the selection of new staff, from outside the organization, you will be involved in selecting people from your existing team for various tasks such as: to join a particular group, for secondment to a special project or to be moved into a different job role, possibly for promotion. Sometimes you will be consulted by your manager about selecting staff from amongst your team, sometimes you will have to make a selection yourself.

Human resource planning

The human resource plan is linked to the business plan. The business plan will indicate how many staff are required and what skills the staff need. The human resource plan is then devised to ensure that the organization has the right number of appropriately skilled people to turn the business plan into reality.

Producing a human resource plan involves:

- forecasting staffing requirements against business objectives
- assessing the available supply of people to meet these requirements
- matching available supply against forecast demand.

Forecasting staffing requirements

By carefully analysing the organization's business plan an informed assessment can be made of future staffing needs. Factors such as a planned re-organization, a change in working patterns such as moving to a system of multi-skilled teams or the introduction of new technology, will have particular significance for future labour demand.

When assessing future staffing requirements, your line manager may approach you to ask for your views; very often you and your line manager will have the best idea of the detailed employment needs in your particular area of the organization; your input can add considerably to the overall accuracy of the forecast.

Assessing available supply

Good personnel records are the key to obtaining information on current employees. A good personnel information system will provide the following information:

- date of birth/age
- sex and race
- disabilities
- education/qualifications
- date of joining company
- job description
- salary/wage
- absence record
- job history, including skills acquired
- promotion and/or performance assessment
- training received.

Investigate 8

How much of the information detailed above is kept in personnel records in your organization?

If good personnel records are maintained, your organization will know, not only how many staff it has, but much more detail which will enable it to assess its staff resources not only in terms of numbers but also in terms of:

- age and sex
- skills, e.g. language, technical or computer capabilities
- educational qualifications
- experience within the company and elsewhere
- performance
- special requirements needed for staff with disabilities
- training requirements
- average length of service
- likely retirements.

It is not only important to have sufficient information about your existing staff, but also to calculate how long your staff are likely to stay with the organization. To do this, labour turnover needs to be analysed.

The simplest way of analysing labour turnover is to use the following formula:

$$\frac{\text{Number of leavers during the year}}{\text{Average numbers employed during the year}} \times 100$$

For example, if an organization employed an average of 150 staff last year and 15 staff left, the labour turnover was

$$\frac{15}{150} \times 100 = 10\%$$

This calculation gives an accurate percentage of labour turnover. It provides a basis on which to estimate the number of current employees who are likely to remain with the organization. The results of the labour turnover calculation can be misleading because there is a tendency for a greater number of new employees to leave the organization soon after joining. For example, in the case of an expanding firm, the formula may show a high labour turnover rate simply because the proportion of newly engaged staff is high. It is therefore useful to calculate the employee stability index, which will indicate the level of retention (and wastage) of the firm's trained workers. This formula is expressed as follows:

$$\frac{\text{Number of employees with 12 months' service or more now}}{\text{Total employed one year ago}} \times 100$$

If we use the same example as above of the 150 employees, 130 have 12 months service or more now and 150 staff were employed one year ago. In this case the stability index is calculated thus:

$$\frac{130}{150} \times 100 = 86.6\%$$

The stability index indicates how successful a firm is in keeping its longer serving and more experienced employees.

Matching supply and demand

You now know the numbers and skills of people that the organization will require for the period of the plan and the likely number of people that will leave the organization. You can move on to compare the demand for, and supply of, labour.

To do this you need to analyse the organization's demand for people and assess if demand can be met from internal resources or if external recruitment is necessary.

If there are likely to be too many employees, action will be needed to balance supply and demand. Your organization may consider increasing the overall level of activity to take up the surplus staff. Where this is not possible, and the surplus occurs in a particular section or part of the organization, it may be possible, with suitable training, to move employees to other areas. Where the problem affects the whole organization, the supply and demand for labour can be brought into balance by reducing or postponing recruitment. As a last resort, staff might have to be made redundant. The easiest way to analyse labour requirements is to construct a chart similar to that shown in Figure 4.2.

If the analysis shows that the organization will need more staff, plans will need to be put in place to recruit sufficient staff to meet demand. We will examine how this is done in the following sections of this chapter.

RECRUITING AND SELECTING YOUR TEAM

Job type	No of staff now	Staff leaving during the year	Promotions to a new job role during the year	Prediction of no of staff in job role after leavers	Total staff required at the end of the year	Total staff required from promotions and recruitment	Anticipated gains from promotions during the year	Total *new* staff required during the year
1	2	3	4	5	6	7	8	9
Senior managers	5	1	–	4	6	2	1	1
Line managers	10	3	1	6	12	6	2	4
Team leaders	20	2	2	16	22	6	5	1
Production staff	100	10	5	85	110	25	–	25
Sales staff	5	–	–	5	6	1	–	1
Office staff	10	–	–	10	12	2	–	2
Totals	150	16	8	126	168	42	8	34

Column 1 gives details of the type of job
Column 2 shows the number of staff employed in the job role now
Column 3 is a prediction based on past experience of labour turnover, of how many staff will leave over the next year
Column 4 shows the number of predicted promotions out of the job role, over the next year
Column 5 shows how many staff will be left after all movements – if no new staff are recruited
Column 6 shows how many staff will be required to achieve the business objectives
Column 7 shows how many staff will be required in new job roles
Column 8 shows anticipated gains from promotions
Column 9 shows the total number of *new* people who need to be recruited into the organization.

Figure 4.2 Analysis of employee requirements

The law and recruitment and selection

If you are involved in any part of the recruitment and selection process, it is important for you to have an awareness of the legal framework as it relates to recruitment practices. The key legislation you need to be aware of is outlined below.

The Sex Discrimination Act 1975
This Act makes discrimination on the grounds of sex or marriage unlawful.

The Race Relations Act 1976
This Act makes the discrimination on the grounds of colour, race, ethnic or national origin unlawful.

Direct and indirect discrimination
Both the Sex Discrimination Act and the Race Relations Act refer to direct and indirect discrimination. Direct discrimination means treating an individual less favourably than another because of their sex, marital status or race. Indirect discrimination occurs when requirements are imposed which are not necessary for the person to do the job and which disadvantage a significantly larger proportion of one sex or racial group than another.

Disability Discrimination Act 1995
The Disability Discrimination Act came into force in December 1996. It applies to employers with more than 20 employees. The Act gives disabled individuals two distinct rights. First, the right not to be discriminated against for a reason which relates to their disability, without justifiable reason. Second, the right to have reasonable adjustments made to premises or working arrangements. Employers need to take care not to discriminate against disabled people at any stage of the recruitment process.

Rehabilitation of Offenders Act 1974
This Act allows people who have been offenders and received a sentence of 30 months or less, to be rehabilitated and their convictions 'spent'. So, after a specified length of time, they can reply 'no' when asked if they have a criminal record. The length of time before a conviction is considered 'spent' varies according to the nature of the conviction and the age of the offender. It is illegal for an employer to discriminate on the grounds of a spent conviction.

Asylum and Immigration Act 1996
This Act made it an criminal offence for an employer to employ someone who does not have permission to live or work in the United Kingdom. It applies to employees who started work for the employer on or after 27 January 1997.

The recruitment and selection process

Figure 4.3 gives a brief explanation of each of the stages in the recruitment and selection process. As you work through the chapter, you will look at each of the stages in more detail.

RECRUITING AND SELECTING YOUR TEAM

What job?	A possible job vacancy is identified. A job analysis is carried out to check that there is definitely a need for a new job. Where there is such a need, job analysis establishes exactly what the job consists of. When this is complete, a job description can be drawn up.

What sort of person?	Now we know what the job is, it is possible to draw up a *person specification* which provides details of the type of person needed to do the job.

Where to look?	Next, a decision has to be made about where to look for the type of person that is required. Where will the job be advertised? Both internal sources and external sources need to be considered.

How to attract candidates?	The *job advertisement* can now be drawn up and placed.

How to choose people to interview	The responses to the job advertisement, usually completed *application forms* and *letters of application* need to be analysed and a short list of the most suitable applicants drawn up.

How to select the right person	One or more selection tools such as an *interview, test(s)* and/or an *assessment centre* are used to select the right person for the job.

Review and evaluation	Conduct a review and evaluation of the process. How did it go? Have you learnt any lessons that will help you do it better next time?

PEOPLE AND SELF MANAGEMENT

Figure 4.3 The recruitment and selection process

What job? – the job analysis and job description

Job vacancies arise in organizations for a variety of different reasons. For example, the organization might be expanding or a member of your workteam might leave because they retire, move out of the area, are promoted or moved to another section.

When it has been decided that there is a vacancy that needs filling in a certain area, the process of job analysis begins. Job analysis is the term used to describe the process of examining a job in order to identify its main features, such as:

• the main duties of the job
• the results the job holder is expected to achieve
• the major tasks undertaken
• the job's relationship with other jobs in the organization.

It is unlikely, as a first line manager, that you will be asked to carry out a job analysis, but you may be asked to contribute to one. It is useful though, to have a list of the tasks that your team carry out, to know how long each task takes and how often it needs to be done.

Activity 18

Conduct a basic analysis of a job carried out by one of your workteam. Keep the analysis safe as you will need it for activities later in this chapter.

The product of a job analysis is a job description. The important questions that need to be answered in order to produce the job description are:

• what is the job title?
• where is the job situated?
• who will the job holder be responsible to?
• what are the main duties of the job holder?
• what responsibilities does the job holder have – for staff, materials, money? What are the consequences of decisions in these areas?
• with whom does the job holder work?
• what are the terms and conditions of the job, hours, overtime, shifts, pay?

The format of job descriptions varies from one organization to another. See Figure 4.4 for a specimen job description.

RECRUITING AND SELECTING YOUR TEAM

Find the job description that relates to the job you analysed in Activity 18. Does the job description match the job analysis you did? Does the job description need updating? Who, within your organization, ought you to inform if the job description is out of date? If there is not a job description for the job you have analysed, devise one.

XYZ Limited

JOB DESCRIPTION

Job Title	Senior Personnel Records Clerk
Responsible to	Personnel Officer
Responsible for	Personnel Records Clerk
(For work direction only)	Office Junior

Main duties

1 Prepares documentation, folders and computer records for new employees including rate cards and details of wages.
2 Salary and wage increases – sends out increase slips to departments, records and checks on return.
3 Keeps records of internal promotions and transfers.
4 Records absence and holiday figures for all employees.
5 Keeps wage rates and salary rates computer records up-to-date.
6 Prepares returns and statistics for Department of Employment and for Personnel Manager and other Personnel Officers.
7 Maintains computer files for all employees.
8 Supervises work of records clerk and office junior.

Other relevant information

The work is in a good modern, airy, office block and general physical conditions are good.
Training will be provided, working with present job holder who is retiring in three months.
Hours: 9.00–5.00 Monday to Friday.
Company sick pay scheme and non-compulsory contributory pension scheme – 3% of salary.
Company discount scheme.
Four weeks holiday per calendar year.
Salary £9500 per annum.

Figure 4.4 A specimen job description. Reprinted by permission of Bankers Books. From *Supervisory Skills* by Sally Palmer (1996).

What sort of person? – the personnel specification

Now you have the details of the vacancy that needs to be filled and a job description for the post. The next thing that you have to decide is what sort of person will be required to carry out the job to an acceptable standard of performance. This is done by drawing up a personnel specification.

The personnel specification is an extremely important feature of the recruitment process, because it sets down the attributes that you are looking for in candidates and provides criteria against which applicants can be assessed.

There are various methods of completing a personnel specification. One of the most commonly used is the seven-point plan, designed by Rodger, which is recommended by the National Institute of Industrial Psychology. The type of person required to do the job is considered under seven headings. A decision is made about which factors are essential for the job holder to carry out their duties and which factors are desirable – but not essential.

The personnel or candidate specification is a summary of the knowledge, skills and personal characteristics required of the job holder to carry out the job to an acceptable standard of performance.

The seven-point plan – *A. Rodger*

1 Physical make-up
2 Attainments
3 General intelligence
4 Special aptitudes
5 Interests
6 Disposition
7 Circumstances.

Figure 4.5 illustrates the factors to consider under each heading of Rodger's seven-point plan.

See Figure 4.6 for a sample personnel specification.

Physical make-up	• What is required in terms of health, strength, energy and personal appearance? • Is appearance, bearing and speech right for the job? • Does the job involve physical strain, is it tiring work? • Does the job involve contact with the public?
Attainments	• What education, training and experience are required? • What type of education? • How well has candidate performed educationally? • What occupational training? • What occupational experience?
General intelligence	• What does the job require in terms of thinking and mental effort? • Does the work call for someone who is specially quick, or can it be done by someone who is average or below average intelligence?
Special aptitudes	• What kind of skills need to be exercised in the job? • Does the work involve an understanding of mechanical things? • Work with figures? • Good oral skills?
Interests	• What personal interests could be relevant to the performance of the job? • Working with people? • Working outdoors? • Making or repairing things?
Disposition	• What kind of personality would be suitable for the job? • Is there an element of leadership in the role? • Does the work need someone who is steady and reliable?
Circumstances	• Are there any special circumstances that the job requires of the candidates? • Will domestic circumstances conflict with the demands of the job?

Figure 4.5 Factors to consider when constructing a personnel specification using Rodger's seven-point plan

	Attribute	Essential	Desirable
1	**Physical make-up**	Weight in proportion to height Good bearing – alert Well dressed, clean appearance Age 25 to 40 Good health – no major disabilities	None
2	**Attainments**	GCSE level Experience of selling in the pharmaceutical industry	Formal training in selling
3	**General intelligence**	Alert, quick thinking	None
4	**Special aptitudes**	Excellent oral communication skills Good command of language Ability to handle objections Ability to handle precise detail Able to listen to customer requirements Ability to build good rapport with customers	Clean driving licence
5	**Interests**	Socializing	Keep fit, sport
6	**Disposition**	Friendly personality Outward looking Persuasive Opportunistic Self starter Team player Ability to work under pressure Enjoy a variety of work Enjoy solving problems Committed to equal opportunities	Sense of humour
7	**Circumstances**	Able to work away from home on a regular basis Able to work long hours when required	Flexible domestic situation

Figure 4.6 A sample personnel specification for a sales representative

Activity 19

You now have enough information to construct or update the job description for the job you analysed in Activity 18. When you have done this, complete the table below to construct a personnel specification for the job.

	Attribute	Essential	Desirable
1	Physical make-up		
2	Attainments		
3	General intelligence		
4	Special aptitudes		
5	Interests		
6	Disposition		
7	Circumstances		

The five-point plan – *J. Munro Fraser*

Another commonly used plan for constructing a person specification is the five-point plan devised by J. Munro Fraser.

1 *Impact on others* – an individual's appearance, speech and manner.

2 *Acquired qualifications* - the knowledge and skills required for the work.
3 *Innate abilities* - the speed and accuracy with which an individual's mind works.
4 *Motivation* - the kind of work that appeals to an individual and how much effort the individual is prepared to apply to it.
5 *Adjustment* - the amount of stress involved in living and working with other people.

Getting approval

Now the job has been analysed and a job description and personnel specification have been devised it is usually necessary to approach a senior manager within the organization who will need to give permission for the job to be created and for the position to be advertised.

Where to look – to attract the right people to apply for the job

Now you have a job description, personnel specification and the necessary approval to proceed, you are ready to attract applicants by taking steps to recruit appropriate staff. As a supervisor you will rarely be involved in this stage of the process, although it is important that you understand the involvement of the personnel department in the overall recruitment and selection process.

People can only apply for a job if they know about it. There are various methods which you can use to recruit staff. Some organizations advertise all vacancies internally before looking outside for new staff; some keep application forms on file from people who have written to the company asking for work when there are no vacancies available. Some organizations use recruitment consultants and many advertise in the press or professional journals. External advertising can be placed in the local press and/or the local job centre, if the type of person you are looking for can be found locally. Many large organizations advertise in the national press and, now that the job market is becoming more global, some advertise in the international press. Trade and professional magazines provide a good forum for recruiting specialists.

RECRUITING AND SELECTING YOUR TEAM

Investigate 10

What are the policies and procedures associated with recruitment in your organization?

Activity 20

Where would you advertise the job that you have analysed and prepared, or updated the job description and personnel specification for, in the previous activities. Why have you selected these methods?

How to attract candidates – the job advertisement

It is important to use the personnel specification to help you word the job advertisement. The job title must be clearly stated and the job location, pay and any additional allowances should be specified. The description of the employing organization must be clear, as must the description of the work that the successful candidate will be expected to undertake and the qualities required. Clear instructions must be given on how to apply, i.e. whether a curriculum vitae should be sent or whether to telephone or write for an application form. Advertisements must not discriminate on the grounds of sex or race. A sample job advertisement is shown in Figure 4.7.

Activity 21

Design a job advertisement for the job you have been working on throughout this chapter.

Investigate 11

Where does your employing organization advertise vacancies? Does it use different methods for different types of jobs? If so, why?

How to choose people to interview

As a first line manager you may be involved in the next stage of the process, which is finding the right person. Most organizations prefer candidates to complete a standard application form. Some also ask for a covering letter and/or a

1. Display advertisements need bold eye-catching headlines. allied to a visually interesting

2. logo or piece of art-work. Notice that this artwork sets a mood of upward success which is not daunting.

3. The Company knows that it is highly regarded so it displays its name prominently to attract high-calibre applicants.

4. The advertisement's title also needs to be displayed prominently

5. This advertisement seizes upon four main 'carrots' to interest the applicant without becoming too detailed or involved. Notice that in this advertisement no 'hard' details are given about pay. hours of work etc.

6. Having conveyed what is on offer. the advertisement briefly sets out the salient features (which are looked for) in an applicant.

7. The name and address of the person to write to are clearly and fully displayed.

8. Note that Smith and Marshall PLC pride themselves on providing equal career opportunities for men and women. The inclusion of this slogan is good public relations as well as an attraction to a wide range of applicants.

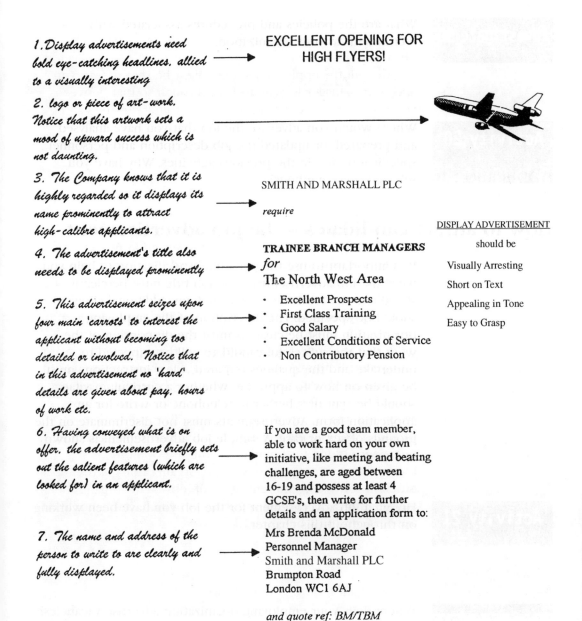

EXCELLENT OPENING FOR HIGH FLYERS!

SMITH AND MARSHALL PLC

require

DISPLAY ADVERTISEMENT
should be
Visually Arresting
Short on Text
Appealing in Tone
Easy to Grasp

TRAINEE BRANCH MANAGERS
for
The North West Area

- Excellent Prospects
- First Class Training
- Good Salary
- Excellent Conditions of Service
- Non Contributory Pension

If you are a good team member, able to work hard on your own initiative, like meeting and beating challenges, are aged between 16-19 and possess at least 4 GCSE's, then write for further details and an application form to:

Mrs Brenda McDonald
Personnel Manager
Smith and Marshall PLC
Brumpton Road
London WC1 6AJ

and quote ref: BM/TBM
SMITH AND MARSHALL PLC
IS AN EQUAL
OPPORTUNITIES
EMPLOYER

Figure 4.7 A sample job advertisement

RECRUITING AND SELECTING YOUR TEAM

curriculum vitae (known as a CV) which is a brief – usually a couple of pages – summary of a person's experience and qualifications. After the Personnel department have collected together all the applications they might be sent to, say, you and your manager for you to look through so that between you a short list of candidates worthy of interviewing can be drawn up.

Application forms

The application form will give you enough information to make a decision about whether or not the applicant is worthy of moving on to the next stage of the selection process, which is usually an interview. The initial information you get from the application form provides evidence of the applicant's suitability or otherwise for the job to be filled.

An applicant who appears to be suitable, at this stage of the process, then becomes a candidate for interview. Most organizations prefer to design their own application forms to require applicants to set out information about themselves in a standardized way. There are two types of application form: a 'closed' application form where only basic information is requested and an 'open' form which asks candidates to provide the basic information, but also asks more searching questions, asking for opinions by the use of more thought-provoking questions. Some organizations have different forms for different types of jobs. Many organizations advise applicants of a closing date, by which time completed applications must be received.

Investigate 12

Get a copy of the application form used by your organization. Is it an open form or a closed form?

Short listing

Following the closing date for applications, it is necessary to move on to the next step in the process: short listing. This is the process of selecting, from the total number of applicants, those who appear from their application form to be worthy of an interview. Short listing should be carried out by more than one person, preferably by the person who will directly supervise the new job holder and that person's manager. If an external advertisement has hit the target segment correctly, there should be some strong candidates for interviewing. It is a good idea when drawing up a short list to divide applications into three groups:

1 *very suitable* - must be interviewed
2 *quite suitable* - call for interview if you have insufficient numbers in category 1, or send a holding letter
3 *not suitable* - send a polite refusal letter, thanking them for their interest in applying for the position.

You can draw up a chart to help you with short listing. Down the left side of the page list all the essential and desirable criteria that you have identified in the personnel specification, as shown in Figure 4.8. Put an identifying name or number for each candidate along the top of the table and construct a chart in which to record your comments.

References

A reference is a brief comment about a candidate which is made by someone who knows the candidate. It is usual practice for a potential employer to ask for the name of two people who can provide a reference for the applicant. Often the application form specifically asks the candidate for their current manager's name for one of the referees. A letter is sometimes sent to the referees requesting a reference for candidates who are short listed or sometimes references are only taken up on the successful candidate following a provisional offer of a job.

How to select the right person

The selection interview

The interview is the most common method of assessing applicants for a job. There are three basic forms to interviews:

1 *the one-to-one interview* - usually with the line manager
2 *the two-to-one interview* - usually with the line manager and another manager or personnel specialist

Essential	Susan	David	Abdul	Irene
Must have 2 years customer service experience	Deals with internal customers in job role 3 yrs	Deals with customers in current job role 4 yrs - sales person	4 yrs working in a customer service job role as customer liaison officer	2 yrs in current job role and 3 yrs in previous job role
Must have at least 1 year supervisory experience	In a supervisory job role for the last 1½ years	Temporary supervisor for 1 year	2 yrs experience in current job role	3 yrs experience in previous job role. (Not supervised a team for the last 2 years)
Good written communication skills	Prepares regular brief reports in current job role. Good letter of application	Prepares weekly sales report. Good letter of application	Well written letter of application. Prepares reports in current job role	Good letter of application
Full, clean driving licence	✓	✓	✓	✓
Computer skills in a Windows environment	Uses Lotus Smartsuite in a Windows environment	Recently trained on a Windows package - but not a regular user	Uses Microsoft Office - Windows environment	Substantial knowledge of a variety of Windows based packages
Able to stay away from home during the week	✓	✓	✓	✓
Desirable				
Knowledge of databases	✗	Some experience of databases	Substantial experience of databases	✗

Figure 4.8 Short listing chart

3 *the panel interview* – usually with a panel of three or more. This type of interview is often used for more senior positions within an organization.

Few managers or supervisors carry out selection interviews regularly and many of them have not received any formal training in the techniques of selection interviewing. It is not surprising that research has shown that selection interviewing is often unreliable. There are two main reasons why so many poor interviews are carried out:

1 lack of training in interview technique
2 lack of adequate preparation for the interview.

If you stick to the guidelines that follow, you will have done your best to ensure that the interview is conducted properly and that you get the best person for the job.

Common interview faults

You need to ensure that you do not stereotype candidates, that is, form an ideal picture of what you think the successful applicant should be like and then match the candidates to your imaginary ideal, rather than evaluating applicants on their merits. This is a particularly common problem when you are replacing a member of the team who did a good job and is leaving; the interviewer can try to match the applicants to the traits that the leaver displayed, not to the criteria that have been set down in the personnel specification.

It is important that you do not make a judgement about the candidate too early in the interview and that you do not pre-judge from the candidate's appearance.

The purpose of the selection interview

During the selection interview you will be aiming to:

• produce a suitable candidate for the job
• provide the candidate with information
• treat all candidates fairly and well.

Preparation for the selection interview

Prepare well for the interview, make sure that you study all the available information such as:

- job description
- person specification
- application form.

When you have done this, prepare an interview plan. Decide what questions you are going to ask the candidates. Make sure that you allow sufficient time for each interview. Check that the room that you will use is appropriate and that you will be free from interruptions.

When the candidates arrive you should do all you can to put them at ease, show them where the toilet facilities are and, if they are going to be waiting, provide refreshments. Ensure that you have explained the structure of the day and that they have somewhere comfortable and private to wait.

If the interview is to be conducted by more than one person make sure that you have met before to decide who is asking what and who will chair the interview panel. Questions should be based mainly around the job description and personnel specification.

Questioning in selection interviewing

It is important to prepare the questions you will ask in advance. Open questions enable the candidate to reply in depth. Open questions begin with what or how or why. They enable a person to reflect on or elaborate upon a particular point in their own way. Examples of open questions are:

- what attracts you to this job?
- why did you leave XYZ company?
- how would you tackle this kind of problem?

Closed questions require a specific answer. They can be asked to confirm information supplied on the application form and to redirect the interview if the candidate is straying off the point. Examples of closed questions are:

- how many people were you responsible for in your last job?
- were you personally authorised to sign purchase orders?
- have you had experience of . . . ?

See Figure 4.9 for examples of open questions.

Activity 22	Rephrase the following closed questions to make them open questions.

Closed question	Rephrased into an open question
Did you enjoy your last job?	
Do you feel you learnt a lot while you were at school?	
Were you attracted to this job because of the salary?	
Do you feel you are qualified for this job?	
Wouldn't you say that you've changed jobs a lot?	
Have you ever had a personality clash with people in that company?	
Were you closely supervised in your last job?	
I've heard that it's a terrible company to work for. Is that true?	
We need someone who can handle a lot of pressure. Can you do that?	

See Feedback section for answers to this activity.

Tell me about . . .

I'd be interested in knowing . . .

How did you feel about . . .

Would you explain . . .

What do you mean by . . .

Please will you clarify . . .

What prompted your decision to . . .

To what do you attribute . . .

Figure 4.9
Open questions

What appealed to you about . . .

Conducting the selection interview

When you have prepared properly, you are ready to conduct the interview. The following guidelines should help:

- welcome interviewee, thank them for coming
- explain the procedure you will adopt for the interview
- start by asking easy, non-threatening questions
- ask open questions
- indicate that you are listening
- make notes when you need to
- listen, watch and ask probing questions
- clamp down, tactfully, on the over-talkative candidate
- keep an eye on the time
- check against the plan that all areas are covered
- give information about the company and the job
- check that the candidate feels that they have had a fair hearing and have no other questions
- advise when an answer can be expected.

Following up the selection interview

Make sure you follow up as soon as possible;

- write up your notes
- decide on the best applicant
- inform applicants of your decision
- arrange for the member of staff to start in their new role.

Tests used in selection

There is a variety of psychological tests that are designed to provide a measure of certain human characteristics. Widely used tests cover such areas as reasoning, intelligence, attainment, occupational preference and personality. The tests have to be administered by specially trained personnel and so organizations usually employ professional psychologists to administer the tests or specially train one or two members of their own staff to administer them.

Assessment centres

An assessment centre is a process which incorporates many forms of assessment. An assessment centre will consist of a variety of activities which candidates have to complete, such as a group activity, discussion, psychological tests, interviews and in-tray exercises. Assessment centres are usually used as a selection tool for the appointment of managers; they have many advantages. A substantial amount of information can be collected about candidates and candidates are given the opportunity to show a range of knowledge and skills. However, assessment centres are very difficult and expensive to set up.

Review and evaluate the selection process

Remember to take some time at the end of any selection process in which you have been involved to reflect on how the whole process went. Are there any lessons you can learn from your experiences? Could you have done anything better? Did any part of the process go particularly well? Review and evaluate the experience and take the opportunity to learn from the process in which you have been involved.

Induction

Now that you have spent considerable time and effort recruiting and selecting a new member of staff, it is important to ensure that you have an induction programme in place which has been designed to help the new employee become familiar with the job and the organization as quickly and easily as possible. Your new employee needs to become familiar with the people, the surroundings, the job, the organization, the sector in which the organization operates and the organization's policies and procedures. See Figure 4.10 for a sample 'induction checklist'.

RECRUITING AND SELECTING YOUR TEAM

Care should be taken not to give the new recruit too much information at one time. Information should be given throughout the induction period.

Induction record

Name of New Entrant _____ Date of Commencement _____

	Carried out by	Date	Comments
1 RECEPTION New employee received by Personnel employment history card completed PAYE slip taken National Insurance Number recorded Introduction to Works and Departmental Manager/Supervisor/Training Instructor/Other staff			
2 TOUR OF SITE Cloakroom and toilets First aid room Lockers Entrances and exits Canteen Notice boards Telephone facilities			
3 THE ORGANISATION Brief history Products or services and markets Organisation structure – branches and departments Future developments			
4 INTRODUCTION TO DEPARTMENT Departmental function, how this relates to rest of organisation New entrant's own job Supervision Colleagues Standard of work expected			
5 CONDITIONS OF EMPLOYMENT Contract of Employment, hours of work including overtime, lunch and tea breaks, periods of notice, written statement of terms Reporting/clocking/flexible working procedures Wage/salary calculation, time of payment; pay statement explained Job grading and evaluation Income Tax, National Insurance and other deductions Holidays Sick leave rules; absence/reporting arrangements Sick pay Pension scheme			
6 POLICIES ON EQUAL OPPORTUNITIES AND EMPLOYEE DEVELOPMENT Training schemes, content and duration Records and progress sheets Further education/training Policy on day/block release			

PEOPLE AND SELF MANAGEMENT

	Carried out by	Date	Comments
Assistance with course fees Performance appraisal Advancement/promotion avenues			
7 SAFETY AND FIRST AID Safety hazards – general; particular to type of work Safety rules Protective clothing, barrier creams Dangers of loose clothing, long hair Housekeeping, tidiness, clear gangways Behaviour – horse-play, jokes Policy on smoking Fires – causes, prevention Location and use of fire-fighting equipment Fire drill and alarm Location of exits Health risks – dangerous substances, processes First aid boxes and procedures Accident reports Safety representatives			
8 ORGANISATION RULES AND PROCEDURES The organisation's rules Misconduct – examples and organisation's response Disciplinary procedures Involvement of employee representatives Grievance procedures Appeals			
9 EMPLOYEE INVOLVEMENT AND COMMUNICATION Trade union recognition Employee or trade union representatives and 'constituencies' Collective agreements and disputes procedures Consultative arrangements Organisation newspapers Communication and briefing arrangements			
10 WELFARE AND EMPLOYEE BENEFITS/FACILITIES Protective clothing – ranges of styles, laundry procedure Safety footwear, styles and sizes, cost and method of payment Medical services Purchase of Company products Suggestions scheme Sports/social facilities Savings scheme Share ownership schemes Transport arrangements			

Reproduced with permission from ACAS Advisory Booklet 'Recruitment and Selection', June 1997.

Figure 4.10 Sample induction checklist

RECRUITING AND SELECTING YOUR TEAM

The induction process is important to the new employee: it will help them to settle down quicker, it also makes good business sense to provide some basic training to your employee so they know a little about the job role and the organization. The induction programme will take less time in a small organization than in a large organization. It is better not to design a programme that is too intensive, it is a good idea to spread the induction over a few days rather than do it in a block.

Summary

Whatever the type of organization it has to be staffed with appropriate people of the right quality. Human resource planning will help to ensure that the organizational needs for human resources are met. Recruitment and selection are vital for all organizations. Although, as a supervisor, you will probably rarely be in a situation where you recruit new starters to the organization, you may be involved in part of the process.

We have looked at the recruitment process, including the need for a job analysis and how a job description and personnel specification are constructed. Carefully written job advertisements placed in the appropriate medium should ensure that a supply of suitable people apply for the job. The successful candidate is selected by using a range of tools, the most commonly used is the interview. It is crucial that interviewers are well prepared prior to the interview.

Review and discussion questions

1 List the stages of the selection process.
2 List five items of information that are usually found in a job description.
3 List the headings that make up the seven-point plan.
4 What should you do to prepare for a selection interview?
5 What should you do to follow up after an interview?
6 Why is it important to provide an induction programme for new starters?

Case study

You are the office supervisor in a factory which manufactures shoes. Business is good and your team of three staff is spending an increasing amount of its time answering the telephone and dealing with visitors to the site. You have discussed this with the General Manager and she has decided that the Company needs a receptionist. This will be a new role within the organization. When you were discussing how to go about filling the new post with the factory manager, Bill, he said, 'Let's appoint Annabel: she's attractive and pleasant, we can easily find someone else to do the job on the production line that she's doing now.'

What is your opinion of Bill's approach to selecting an appropriate person for the new receptionist's job?

What method would you suggest for recruiting and selecting the appropriate person for this specific post?

Work-based assignment

C7.1
C7.2

Conduct an investigation into the human resource planning, recruitment and selection procedures used by your organization. Using the following headings, write a paragraph for each heading explaining the process used by your organization. Support your work with sample documentation from your organization.

Section 1 Human Resource Planning
Section 2 Recruitment

- recruitment policy
- job analysis
- job description
- personnel specification
- approval for the new job
- the job advertisement

Section 3 Selection

- the selection tools used
- the people involved

Section 4 How the recruitment and selection process in my organization could be improved

5 Leading your team

Learning objectives

On completion of this chapter you will be able to:

- explain the importance and meaning of leadership
- differentiate between leadership and management
- list the qualities of a good leader
- describe the difference between leadership and power
- describe Adair's 'Action-centred' functional approach to leadership
- describe a range of management styles
- define delegation
- differentiate between delegation, dumping, abdication and telling people what to do
- appreciate the difference between simple and complex delegation
- understand the benefits and risks of delegation
- explain how to delegate successfully.

Introduction

The most important aspect of your job as a team leader is to work with management to direct the efforts of the members of your team towards the achievement of organizational objectives. You will do this by doing all that you can to ensure that your team achieves its targets and meets its objectives. It is therefore worth spending some time considering the factors which will help to create a successful relationship between you and your team. In this chapter we will consider whether leadership and management are the same thing. We will look at what makes a good leader, ask whether leadership can be learnt, the relationship between leadership and power, and a number of approaches to leadership. We also examine delegation in this chapter.

Management and leadership

Activity 23

Is there a difference between leadership and management?

We looked at the managerial aspects of a team leader's role in Chapter 1. You will remember they were setting objectives, planning, organizing, coordinating, motivating, communicating, monitoring, controlling and evaluating. Leadership is related to many aspects of management; a good leader will find it much easier to be a better manager, but there are differences between leadership and management.

Not every leader is a manager and not every manager is a leader. Some people are leaders when they do not have a formal leadership role within an organization. This is because they display leadership qualities. Leadership is about motivating and encouraging participation and involvement, it is about relationships with people. Management is about getting things done through other people, it is about planning, organizing, directing and controlling the activities of the workteam. If you want to be an effective team leader it is important to understand the concept of leadership; a good team leader is a good leader of people (as the job title 'team leader' implies), as well as a good manager.

Can leadership be learnt?

Activity 24

Which of the two statements below do you believe are correct?

'People are born with leadership qualities, some people are natural leaders, they are born to lead. Others do not have the qualities to make a good leader and never will have.'

'Leadership can be learnt, if a person wants to be a leader they can learn how to be a leader, just like it is possible to learn other skills at work.'

Some people do naturally have more leadership qualities than others but it is possible to learn the skills of leadership. Many leaders in successful organizations today started at the bottom of the organization and worked their way up, learning as they went. They were not all outstanding leaders when they first started work.

The qualities of a good leader

Good leaders do possess certain qualities; if we know what the qualities are we can work towards being a good leader.

Activity 25

List five great leaders.

See Feedback section for answer to this activity.

Activity 26

Think about the five leaders that you listed in Activity 25. List ten qualities that all the five leaders displayed, qualities that in your opinion made them all good leaders.

It is not difficult to believe that many writers have made a study of the qualities that combine to make a good leader. Your list will not be the same as the list in Figure 5.1, but it is likely that you will have listed some very similar qualities. Most people seem to agree that good leaders should have the qualities listed in Figure 5.1.

Leadership and power

Power is a factor in leadership and in organizations, people use power to get things done. To have power is to have the ability to influence people and events. Within an organization, leadership influence will be dependent upon the type of power that the leader can exercise over other people. Five main sources of power which individuals develop or acquire are shown in Figure 5.2. These five sources of power are based on what the subordinate perceives the influence of the leader to be. For example, if a person believes that a manager in a different department has authority over them, whether the manager does or not there is perceived legitimate power.

1 Drive and enthusiasm	The desire and energy to get on with the job. Enthusiasm rubs off on the whole team so does the lack of it
2 Honesty and integrity	Sticking to your values. Without integrity you are not likely to be successful. Integrity is essential to gain the trust and confidence of your team
3 Reliability and dependability	Never letting the team down
4 Fairness	A good team leader is fair minded and impartial at all times. It is about not taking sides and dealing with everyone fairly
5 Communication skills	The ability to communicate is an essential skill which you must develop if you are to be a good leader. It is essential that you understand the people around you and that you are understood. It is important to be a good listener
6 People skills	Having a genuine interest in people, liking them and wanting to help and develop them
7 Ability to make difficult decisions	Before making any decision get all the facts and discuss with everybody concerned: your team, other team leaders, your manager. When things go wrong, take time to get the facts and weigh up the situation. A good leader has good judgement
8 Confidence	In yourself and your team
9 Vision	The ability to see the 'big' picture and look ahead
10 Sense of humour	This is very valuable, a sense of humour keeps things in proportion. Good team leaders are occasionally prepared to laugh at themselves

Figure 5.1 The qualities of a good leader

Charismatic power	This power stems from the personal magnetism that attracts people to them.
Legitimate power	This type of power is based on the position that the person has in the organization. Legitimate power is based on authority.
Expert power	This is based on the specialized knowledge that is possessed by the individual.
Reward power	This type of power is based on the ability that the leader has to obtain rewards for those who comply with directives, for example, pay, promotion, praise and recognition.
Coercive power	This is based on fear and the subordinate feeling that the leader has the ability to punish people who do not comply.

Figure 5.2 Sources of power. Adapted from French and Raven

LEADING YOUR TEAM

Activity 27

Consider each of the different types of power above.
Complete the following chart.

Type of power	A situation when somebody used this type of power to influence me	How I felt about it
Charismatic		
Legitimate		
Expert		
Reward		
Coercive		

Use this activity to reflect upon how you use your power and the effect that is has on the people you work with.

Types of leadership

Functional leadership

John Adair set down his ideas on 'action-centred leadership'. This approach focuses attention on the functions of leadership and believes that leadership skills can be learnt. Adair believes that leadership is more a question of appropriate behaviour than of personality. He stated that the effectiveness of the leader is dependent upon meeting three areas of need within the work group, the need to:

- *task functions (needs)* – define and achieve the common task
- *team functions (needs)* – build and maintain the team
- *individual functions (needs)* – satisfy and develop the individuals within the team.

Adair's model is shown in Figure 5.3. You can see that Adair symbolizes the three functions by three overlapping circles.

The items you should be considering to ensure that you meet the needs of the task, the team and the individuals are detailed in Figure 5.4.

Figure 5.3
Action-centred
leadership –
John Adair.
Reprinted by
permission of Gower
Publishing. From
Effective Leadership
(1983) by John Adair

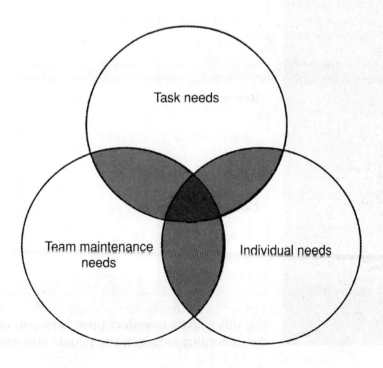

Task needs

Team maintenance
needs

Individual needs

Task functions involve:

- achieving the objectives of the work group
- defining group tasks
- planning the work
- allocating resources
- organizing duties and responsibilities
- controlling quality and checking performance
- reviewing progress.

Team functions involve:

- maintaining morale and building team spirit
- the cohesiveness of the group as a working unit
- setting standards and maintaining discipline
- systems of communication within the group
- training the group
- appointment of sub-leaders.

Individual functions involve:

- meeting the needs of the individual members of the group
- attending to personal problems
- giving praise and status
- reconciling conflicts between group needs and needs of the individual
- training the individual.

Figure 5.4 The supervisor's considerations in action-centred leadership

Adair also said that there were essential leadership actions:

- defining the objective
- planning
- communicating
- supporting/controlling
- informing
- evaluating.

Figure 5.5 illustrates the actions and how the leader's actions can meet task, team and individual needs. An effective leader satisfies all three interrelated areas of need.

Action-centred leadership

Actions by the leader	Task	Team	Individual needs
1 Define objective	Identify the problems and tasks Identify constraints Obtain all available information	Set targets 'Involve' the staff Create team spirit	Assess individual skills Examine your training programme Set targets
2 Plan	Establish your resources and priorities Make your decisions	Examine structure and job allocation Delegate	Agree individual targets Agree personal responsibilities Delegate
3 Communicate	Brief the staff Check their understanding of your briefing	Have regular consultation with staff Obtain and examine the feedback Test ideas	Listen to the staff – ideas and troubles Give advice when necessary Show enthusiasm Examine your own attitudes
4 Support/control	Monitor progress being made Check to see that your standards are being maintained	Co-ordinate the work Reconcile any conflict	Recognize and give encouragement Counsel
5 Evaluate	Review the task and your functions Re-plan and carry forward incomplete targets if necessary	Acknowledge and reward success Learn from any failure Inform staff of results	Personal appraisal Give guidance and encouragement Examine personal needs for further training

Figure 5.5 Actions by the leader in action-centred leadership

The style approach to leadership

A person's leadership style is the pattern of behaviour they exhibit in carrying out a leadership role.

Autocratic versus democractic

The most common division of styles is between autocratic (or authoritarian) and democratic. One of the most well-known models of leadership style was devised by Tannenbaum and Schmidt. They suggested that there is a range of possible leadership styles available to a manager, as shown in Figure 5.6.

In Figure 5.6, you can see that the further to the right, the model is increasingly democratic and subordinates within the organization are given increasingly more freedom to make decisions for themselves. This approach can be seen as identifying four main styles of leadership by the manager.

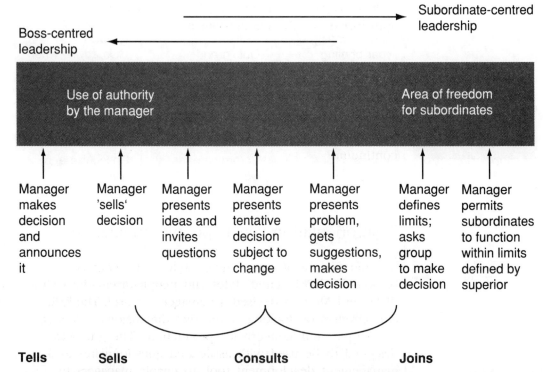

Figure 5.6 Continuum of leadership behaviour – *Tannenbaum and Schmidt*. Reprinted by permission of *Harvard Business Review* (an exhibit). From 'How to choose a leadership pattern' by Robert Tannenbaum and Warren H. Schmidt, May–June 1973. Copyright © 1973 by the President and Fellows of Harvard College. All rights reserved.

PEOPLE AND SELF MANAGEMENT

- *Tells* – the manager identifies the problem, chooses a decision and announces this to subordinates, expecting them to implement it without an opportunity for participation
- *Sells* – the manager still chooses the decision but recognizes the possibility of some resistance from those affected by the decision and attempts to persuade subordinates to accept it
- *Consults* – the manager identifies the problem but does not choose a decision until the problem is presented to the group and the manager has listened to advice and solutions suggested by subordinates
- *Joins* – the manager defines the problem and limits within which the decision must be made and then passes it to the group (with the manager as a member) to make the decision.

The continuum shows a range of leadership styles ranging from boss centred, very autocratic, to a very 'hands off', laissez faire approach. There is no one best style. The skill of a manager is to adopt the style which is most appropriate for the circumstances.

Activity 28

Consider your own management style and that of your line manager. Where would you place your style and that of your manager on Tannanbaum and Schmidt's continuum?

Task orientation versus people orientation

Another feature of management style is the contrast between task-orientated styles and people-orientated styles. Blake and Mouton devised a management grid. The grid concentrates on looking at the two dimensions of 'concern for people' and 'concern for production'. The grid was designed to be used with associated questionnaires as a management development tool, to enable managers to assess their own management style and think about adjusting their style to become more effective. The grid is shown in Figure 5.7.

LEADING YOUR TEAM

88

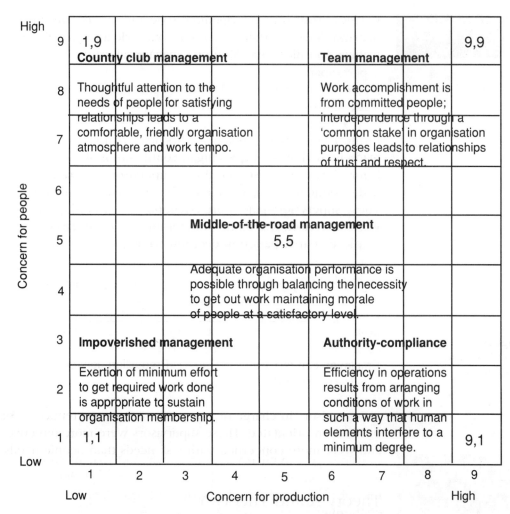

Figure 5.7 Managerial grid – *Blake and Mouton*. From *Leadership Dilemmas – Grid Solutions*, p. 29, by Robert R. Blake and Anne Adams McCanse. Copyright © 1991 by Robert R. Blake and the estate of Jane S. Mouton. Used with permission. All rights reserved

The five styles marked on the grid are:

9.9 'Team management' The ideal style. High production is achieved by integrating task and human requirements.

1.9 'Country Club' Too much concern for people, very little gets done.

9.1 'Task' Too concerned with production, people are treated like machines.

1.1 'Impoverished' No concern for people or output.

5.5 'Middle-of-the-road' Push for production, but do not go all out. Give some but not all.

Consider your own management style and that of your line manager. Where would you place your style and that of your manager on Blake and Mouton's managerial grid?

The Michigan continuum

In the 1950s a study of supervisors' leadership styles was made in Michigan. The Michigan continuum is shown in Figure 5.8. It was discovered that supervisors in charge of high-producing groups tended to be employee-orientated. These supervisors paid more attention to relationships at work, exercised less direct supervision and encouraged employee participation in decision-making.

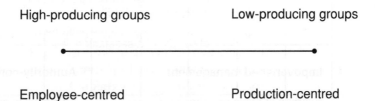

Figure 5.8
The Michigan continuum

Supervisors in charge of low producing groups tended to be production orientated. These supervisors were more directive and were more concerned with task needs than people needs.

Theory X and Theory Y

Douglas McGregor's Theory X, Theory Y approach illustrates very well the differences between a people-orientated approach to people at work and a production-orientated approach. McGregor developed two sets of assumptions that managers could have about their workers.

Theory X

The Theory X manager believes that workers:

• dislike work and responsibility and prefer to be told what to do
• work for money, not the desire to do a good job
• need to be closely supervised and controlled or they will not achieve the objectives of the organization.

LEADING YOUR TEAM

McGregor said that if managers treated people as if they were Theory X type, that is how they would behave, so the Theory X team leader will have people in their team that require close supervision.

Theory Y

The Theory Y manager believes that workers:

- will enjoy their work if you provide opportunities for them to exercise control over their own work and performance
- are not just concerned with financial rewards, they also want to mix with their co-workers and do a good job
- will work better and more productively if supervision is kept to a minimum and if they are allowed to make decisions for themselves.

The Theory Y approach was based on a humane approach to management. McGregor proposed that if workers were treated in this way, they would respond to this and behave in the way the Theory Y manager expected.

In essence McGregor was saying that if you expect the best from employees they will respond in kind.

Activity 30 | Consider your management style and that of your line manager. Do you lean towards Theory X or Theory Y?

Management by walking about

Management by walking about (MBWA) proposes that it is not possible for a manager to be effective sitting in his/her office all day. An effective manager needs to literally walk about the place. This will show an interest in the work of the whole team, make the manager accessible to hear about the problems of team members and keep the manager in close contact with the workforce.

Delegation

Delegation occurs when a manager (delegator) gives a subordinate (delegatee) additional *responsibility* for a certain task and the *authority* to get the job done, whilst retaining

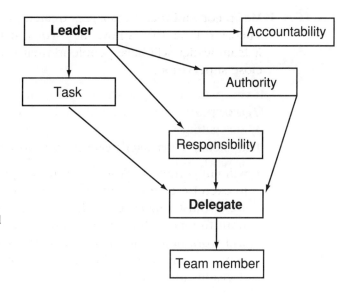

Figure 5.9
Delegation. Reprinted
by permission of
Bankers Books. From
Supervisory Skills by
Sally Palmer (1996)

overall *control* for the outcome, and *accountability* for the
result. You can only delegate a task if you give the person to
whom you are delegating the necessary powers to carry out
the task properly. It is important, when you are delegating, to
remember to give your staff the necessary information to do
the job and to make sure that they know the standards that
have to be met. For delegation to be successful it has to be
well planned and you will have to invest time, effort and
training. See Figure 5.9 for a diagram illustrating delegation.
Delegation is not telling people what to do, nor is it
abdication which is a failure to take any responsibility or
which is getting rid of the boring parts of your work.

Types of delegation

Simple delegation

Simple delegation is looking at what people do and giving
them the responsibility for their existing job.

Complex delegation

Complex delegation is also known as true delegation. It is
giving one of your team part of what is truly your job and the
responsibility and authority they need to carry out the task.

The benefits of delegation

More effective use of your time

If you plan carefully what you are going to delegate you can fill the gap in your work with higher level management work. By delegating you can spend more time on taking an overview, initiating and planning and on the creative areas of your work. You can also free yourself from interruptions as your staff will have the authority to work on their own, unsupervised.

Motivation of staff

Delegation will increase the involvement, interest and challenge of your subordinate's job. By giving your staff more responsibility they will gain increased job satisfaction, valuable experience, improved motivation, and higher self-esteem. Overall performance will improve, their prospects for promotion will also improve.

Training

Delegation is a type of on-the-job training. By delegating you are giving your team new experiences and teaching them new skills.

Self-development

Delegation will give you the opportunity to spend your time on less routine tasks so that you can improve your own skills and develop new ones.

A more effective working team

By spreading the workload your team will develop a much greater understanding of a wide range of aspects of the work of your section. This will improve team working and the overall quality of the work of the team will improve.

PEOPLE AND SELF MANAGEMENT

How to delegate successfully

Successful delegation has to be planned. It should form part of the overall plan that you have to develop both yourself and your workteam. It will fit into your plans to improve the way in which your team works together, to improve the quality of service that you provide by ensuring that jobs can always be covered if a member of the team is absent and that the staff understand more fully the work of your section.

Planning delegation

Deciding what can be delegated, to whom and what training will be required.

Identify suitable opportunities for delegation:

- do this by analysing your job
- list all the tasks that need to be done
- estimate the time required for each task
- decide on those tasks which could be delegated, i.e. it would benefit you to lose them and benefit your staff to do them
- choose what you do yourself and what you delegate
- if you choose all the most interesting jobs for yourself, you will be dumping, not delegating, and you will not motivate your staff
- delegate carefully selected more challenging work in order to motivate and develop your staff.

Identify suitable staff to whom to delegate:

- do this by looking at the workload of your team, do they have time to take on extra work?
- what skills do they have?
- do they have skills that you are not utilizing?
- have they shown an interest in developing their skills further?
- will they enjoy the extra tasks that you have in mind?
- assess the capabilities of your workteam, bearing in mind that it is part of your role to provide them with opportunities for further development.

Train the delegatee:

- the person that you have selected to do the task may not be able to do it until you provide the appropriate training

- select the appropriate training which might be on-the-job or off-the-job.
- discuss this with the person to whom you are delegating to ensure that they understand the reason for the training.

Activity 31

Analyse your job using the model given above. Identify suitable opportunities for delegation:

Analyse your job, by listing the tasks that you do and estimating the time required for each task	List the tasks that make up your job here
Decide on those tasks which could be delegated, i.e. it would benefit you to lose them and benefit your staff to do them You have to choose what you do yourself and what you delegate Remember: if you choose all the most interesting jobs for yourself, you will be dumping not delegating and you will not motivate your staff. You need to delegate carefully selected more challenging work in order to motivate and develop them	List here the tasks you have chosen to delegate

Identify suitable staff to whom to delegate:

Analyse the workload of your team, do they have time to take on extra work?	
What skills do they have?	
Do they have skills that you are not utilizing?	
Have they shown an interest in developing their skills further?	
Will they enjoy the extra tasks that you have in mind?	
Assess the capabilities of your workteam, bearing in mind that it is part of your role to provide them with opportunities for further development	

Consider how you will train the delegatee. The person that you have selected to do the task may not be able to do it until you provide the appropriate training. Select the appropriate training which might be on-the-job or off-the-job.

The next stage is to discuss the proposed training with the person to whom you are delegating to ensure that they understand the reason for the training.

Applying delegation

Briefing the delegatee carefully and giving the authority and resources to do the tasks.

Match the tasks to the appropriate member of the team. Brief the delegatee carefully, then allocate the task:

* explain what has to be done
* explain what results and standards are required
* explain the bounds of responsibility that you are delegating
* explain what authority the delegatee has
* explain how the delegatee will benefit
* brief other people on the responsibility and authority that have been given.

Controlling delegation

Keeping an eye on what is happening and making time to check everything is as it should be. Encouraging and supporting the delegatee.

Control and feedback:

* show confidence in the person to whom you have delegated
* be available to give guidance
* control by checking performance – but do not interfere
* give constructive feedback on a regular basis
* if all is going well, do not forget to praise good work.

The risks of delegation

Some managers do not delegate because of the risks of delegation. The risks are outlined below.

Lack of confidence in subordinates

Some people do not have sufficient faith in their subordinates to delegate. However, it is part of the supervisor's job to develop the abilities of their team and this can only be achieved by giving them more responsibility. If delegation is properly planned and controlled the subordinate will not do too much damage if things start to go wrong, because you will have a mechanism in place for checking their progress.

Fear

There are two main reasons for fear. Firstly, some managers prefer not to delegate because they are afraid of losing control and that their subordinates will take over their job. However, if you delegate properly, you have the opportunity to increase your control, gain the respect of your staff and improve efficiency. Secondly, some managers fear that their subordinates might do a better job than them, but it is not a competition, it is the manager's job to get the best out of their team. The person that is doing the delegated task(s) is not doing all of your job, surely you can cope if they are better at one aspect of it than you are.

Worry that team members will not accept the delegated tasks

Some staff do not wish to accept the opportunity to do delegated tasks. This can be for many reasons. Sometimes they are frightened of making mistakes because of their manager's attitude to errors or because they are lacking in confidence. Subordinates will shy away from extra responsibility if they have not been adequately trained. Some will not take on more responsible tasks as they are content with their current work role – they do not want any extra responsibility or they will not take on any extra responsibility without extra reward. These are difficult situations to deal with: a person will need reassuring and to have the advantages, to themselves and their team, of undertaking the delegated work spelled out. In the final analysis you do have the power to tell them what to do, but you may not wish to use this if it will upset the atmosphere within your workteam, especially as you may be asking them to do a task which is outside their normal job role.

Indispensability

Many managers consider themselves indispensable, believing that they are the only people capable of performing certain activities or making particular decisions. If you try to do everything yourself you will be an ineffective manager and so be more likely to be dispensable.

Concern about what to do with the extra time

If you are delegating part of your work you will have more time to do the things mentioned on page 92, where we listed the benefits of delegation, all of which should improve your performance and the team's performance. Surely that will fill the extra time created and justify your role within the organization.

Summary

There is no one best style of leadership, although research has shown that democratic and participative styles of leadership generally encourage more effective workteams. The most appropriate style for the leader to adopt will depend on the situation and the people involved. An effective leader gains the commitment and cooperation of the work group. This is more likely to be achieved by a leader who is concerned about people and who displays a human relations approach which should lead to a satisfied, high producing and cohesive team.

Review and discussion questions

1 Distinguish leadership from management.
2 'Never mind what people say; leaders are made, not born.' What does the speaker mean by this? Do you agree? How would you help a member of your team who had to take on leadership responsibilities?
3 What are the qualities of a good leader?
4 What did Adair describe as the three functions of leadership?
5 Draw Tannenbaum and Schmidt's continuum of leadership behaviour.

6 Describe the following leadership styles: tells, sells, consults and joins.
7 What are the five styles of leadership behaviour described by Blake and Mouton?
8 Draw a diagram to illustrate the Michigan continuum.
9 Describe five sources of power.
10 Is there one best style of leadership?
11 Define delegation.
12 What is the difference between delegation and dumping?
13 Describe simple and complex delegation.
14 List the benefits of delegation.
15 Why is it important to plan delegation carefully?
16 How do you identify opportunities for delegation?
17 How do you match a delegated task to a suitable delegatee?
18 What information would you include in a delegation briefing to a member of your team?
19 Why is it important to control delegation?
20 Describe the risks associated with delegation. If supervisors wish to delegate, how can they minimize the effects of those risks?

Case study A colleague of yours, Simon, is in a job role similar to yours: you are both team leaders. He tells you that he is having problems with his workteam because 'they will not do as they are told'. Simon says that he cannot understand what their problem is, 'people should do what the team leader tells them to do, they should obey those who are in authority'. Why do you think Simon is experiencing problems with his team? What advice would you give him?

Work-based assignment

C12.1
C12.2

Complete the following action plan.

Question	Guidance notes	Action plan
1 Are you confident that you have all the skills you require to be a good team leader?	If you need to develop in some skill areas, specify what they are, decide what you are going to do about it	
2 Is everyone in your team clear about the role of the team within the organization? Are they all clear about what you are working to achieve?	If not, what do you need to do about it? How will you go about clarifying the team's role and goals for the benefit of team members?	
3 Do you do sufficient planning?	If the answer is no, try making more detailed plans, spend more time planning	
4 Is your team well motivated?	If motivation could be improved, what action can you take?	
5 Do you communicate well with your team?	Could you improve your communication skills? If so, what particular aspects do you need to improve?	
6 Do you provide your team with all the support they need?	Do you need to improve the support that you provide to your team? How will you do this?	
7 Do you represent your team well to management?	Are you sufficiently loyal to your team?	
8 Do you ensure that you meet the needs of all the members of your team?	What motivates your team members? Do you provide them with all the support and encouragement they need?	
9 Do you get your team involved with planning and organizing work and contributing to decision making?	Ask your team. Do you need to improve in this area?	
10 Could your team's relationships with other teams be better?	If the answer to this question is yes, what can you do about it? How will you build better links with other teams?	

Now you have formulated your action plan, record your progress against your action plan for three months on a monthly basis.

6 Training and developing your team

Learning objectives

On completion of this chapter you will be able to:

- identify what is meant by appraisal
- explain the purpose of appraisal
- list the features of a good appraisal system
- appreciate how to conduct an appraisal interview
- explain the term 'reward review'
- differentiate between training, development and education
- appreciate why staff need training
- understand the team leader's role in training
- define the term 'training gap'
- differentiate between on-the-job and off-the-job training
- explain the advantages and disadvantages of different types of training
- understand how to plan and control training
- state the advantages of training to the trainee and the organization.

Introduction

A good team leader sees the development of their team as a key task. The most important resource that any organization has is its people. It is their performance that determines the ability of the organization, and your team within the organization, to achieve the organizational objectives and team objectives. In this chapter we will look at the team leader's involvement in the process of identifying training and development needs and providing the training and development identified.

The purpose of appraisal

Staff appraisal is an important tool that managers can use to help improve the performance of the individuals that make up their teams.

Appraisal has several purposes:

- to gather information about the skills and potential of existing employees
- to assess the performance of employees
- to let employees know how well they have performed and to provide an assessment of their strengths and areas for development
- to allow the person being appraised and their team leader to discuss how they can achieve their personal objectives and the job objectives.

Staff appraisal is any procedure which helps the collecting and sharing of information about people and the use of that information to add to their performance at work. Appraisals regularly record an assessment of an employee's performance, potential and development needs. In addition, the appraisal system may be used to determine whether employees should receive an element of financial reward for their performance.

The two key features of appraisal are:

- *assessment* – of team members' performance
- *feedback* – to team members' on their performance.

Every organization has a different appraisal system. You will be familiar with the system used by your organization. When you work through this unit it would be beneficial for you to have a copy of your last appraisal in front of you. It will then be possible for you to relate the content of this unit to your own organization's system and to your personal experiences of appraisal.

Training and developing your team is an important part of your role; if you ensure that your team is properly trained they will be motivated and the output and quality of work will be high.

The features of a good appraisal system

Every appraisal system needs:

- senior managers to be committed to appraisal
- a straightforward system which everybody understands, without too much complicated paperwork
- openness and trust in a well-defined system

- development of appraisal skills through training, so that appraisals are conducted in a professional manner
- action as a result of appraisal or people will lose faith in the system
- monitoring of the system to check it is working properly.

| **Activity 32** | How does your appraisal system measure up? Complete the following chart for your own appraisal system. |

Conditions of a good appraisal system	✓
Senior managers are committed to appraisal	
It is a straightforward system which everybody understands, without too much complicated paperwork	
There is openness and trust in a well defined system	
People receive development of appraisal skills through training	
Appraisals are conducted in a professional manner	
There is action as a result of appraisals	
The appraisal system is monitored to check it is working properly	

Whatever the appraisal system used, appraisals usually take place once per year, but the frequency will vary from organization to organization. It is usual for the appraisal documentation to be seen by the appraisee and for the appraisee to sign the final report to signify their agreement to the content of the appraisal report. Some systems require the appraisee to make a comment on the final report.

The job role of the person who carries out the appraisal will vary from system to system. The appraiser is usually the appraisee's immediate line manager but, in some organizations, the appraisal will be carried out by a more senior manager. In most cases a senior manager and the personnel department look at the appraisal when it has been completed. This enables senior management and personnel to check progress and be aware of who is ready for promotion and who has a training need.

The design of the appraisal forms will vary from organization to organization. However, most performance appraisal forms contain the following information:

- basic personal details, i.e. name, department, post, length of time in job
- job title
- job description
- a detailed review of the individual's performance against a set of job-related criteria
- an overall performance rating
- general comments by a more senior manager
- comments by the employee
- a plan for development and action.

The benefits of an appraisal system

A good appraisal system has many benefits:

- appraisals can help to improve employee performance and to reveal problems that may be restricting the employee's progress and causing inefficient work practices
- they provide information for human resource planning and help to determine the employee's suitability for promotion and training
- appraisals also improve communications by giving the appraisee a chance to talk about their ideas and expectations.

Potential problems with an appraisal system

There can be problems with appraisal and managers need to take care that the following problems do not occur:

- *the halo or horns effect* – this is where one characteristic of the appraisee excessively influences the appraiser's ratings on all factors. For example, if the appraiser decides that the appraisee is particularly good in one important aspect of their work and gives unjustifiably high ratings to all areas of that person's work (halo effect). Or if the employee has one serious fault and the appraiser allows that to influence all other ratings (horns effect)

- *Variations in reporting standards* – some appraisers might be generally over-generous or generally over-critical. A good monitoring system and the fact that senior managers see reports should help to overcome this.
- *Emphasis on the recent past* – most appraisals report on a period of one year, some managers might find it difficult to recall the events of the past year. It is a good idea for the manager to keep a log of significant events for each member of staff.

The appraisal interview

Your role in the appraisal system within your organization will vary from one organization to another. You will probably be consulted regarding the appraisal of your team members even if you do not conduct the appraisal interviews yourself. You need to be fully aware of the performance of each member of your team so that you can make a valid contribution to the appraisal process. For those of you who are involved in appraisal interviewing some guidance is given below.

The aim of the appraisal interview is:

- to review past performance as a basis for training and development.
- to set goals for the next period and to establish means of making progress.

By the end of the interview, the appraisee needs to know the answers to the following questions:

- how well am I doing?
- where can I improve?
- what can I do well?
- what help do I need to improve?
- what are my goals for the next period?
- what is the action plan to achieve them?

Before the interview

Allow time for you and the appraisee to prepare for the interview, give a couple of weeks notice of the date of the interview. When you are preparing for the interview, consider the objectives of the interview, which are:

- to assess performance
- to decide how to build on strengths
- to identify areas of improvement, ways of overcoming weaknesses and consequent training needs
- to discuss potential for future development, achievements during the year, changes in circumstances, changes in the job description, relationships at work and potential opportunities for self-development.

Always arrange for a private room with an informal setting to conduct the interview.

During the interview

- State objectives of the interview, stress the two-sided nature of the interview
- listen and ask questions
- concentrate on performance not personality
- be specific about success or failures
- agree objectives and action plans
- do not be destructive
- hold a 'purposeful chat' rather than an 'inquisition'.

After the interview

- Complete the forms
- take any action agreed
- monitor progress
- follow up any issues.

Giving feedback

However good the appraisal system is, it is not a replacement for providing your team members with regular feedback. Feedback is a continuous process by which people let us know about the effects of our actions. They may do this consciously, by telling us how they feel or unconsciously, by changing their behaviour towards us, which you may or may not notice. As a team leader it is important that you can both receive and give feedback. We will concentrate here on looking at how you can give feedback to your workteam.

We have already established that most organizations have an appraisal system which enables managers and team leaders to feed back to their team members. But feedback is much more than this: it should not only happen at appraisals, it should be ongoing. Feedback is much more effective if it is given directly after an event and not dealt with at the annual appraisal.

Positive and negative feedback

Positive feedback is easy to give. It is about congratulating somebody for a job well done. It is one of the best methods of motivating your team and so improving or maintaining high performance. The problem with positive feedback is that all too often we forget to do it.

Negative feedback is when you need to talk to a person, usually one of your team, about poor performance. You need the person to change their behaviour so that they will do a better job in the future. Giving feedback to your team is the best method of improving their performance, but you must be careful not to undermine and demoralize your team member by giving feedback insensitively or with insufficient thought or preparation.

Feedback and criticism

Feedback is not the same as criticism. Feedback is positive and criticism is negative. Feedback and criticism are contrasted in Figure 6.1.

Guidelines for giving feedback

One of the problems with feedback is that we, managers, are often very uncomfortable about giving it.

You need to overcome concerns that you may have about giving feedback. You will be able to do this if you and your

Feedback	Criticism
Focuses on incident that occurred	Focuses on the person
Looks to the future and how it is possible to improve	Looks to the past
Looks for joint solutions to problems	Allocates blame
Makes specific comments	Makes generalizations
Approaches the session in a positive, friendly manner	Approaches the session in a hostile or aggressive manner

Figure 6.1
The differences between feedback and criticism

team believe that feedback is a positive process. If you give feedback honestly, specifically and sensitively, feedback will improve performance.

You need to handle giving feedback very carefully. You must not be aggressive or angry. Before you give feedback you must be clear about exactly what you want to achieve. You will probably want to agree some outcomes with the person you are talking to. Be clear about these. Write them down. You must be clear about the message that you want to give to the person. You also need to decide how you want to conduct the session; you must give the person you are speaking to an opportunity to present their own viewpoint, listen carefully and yet ensure that you achieve the outcome you need.

There are five key steps which will make giving feedback easy:

1 maintain the other person's self esteem
2 feedback as soon as possible after the event
3 feedback in relation to the specific event
4 discuss why it was not good
5 decide together a better way of doing it.

See Figure 6.2 for more detail on giving feedback.

Maintain the other person's self esteem
Take a positive approach. The person can improve their
performance in this area. Make sure the person understands
why it was not good enough and the benefits of overcoming
the problem. Ensure that they understand that you value
them as a person. Be friendly, confident and enthusiastic.

Feedback as soon as possible after the event
It is important not to delay. The sooner the better. The
incident is fresh in both your minds. You will be less likely to
put it off and possibly not do it at all!

Feedback in relation to the specific event
Only feedback on one event. Do not take the opportunity to
deal with any other issues.

Discuss why it was not good
Listen to what the other person has to say. Talk about how
you felt about it. Deal with what happened, not the
personalities.

Decide together a better way of doing it
Discuss how the person can improve. Ask them for
suggestions. What can be done to improve? Be positive.
Offer support.

Figure 6.2
Giving feedback

Reward reviews

Performance appraisal systems can motivate and improve
performance. However, in some organizations, systems are
being introduced that link rewards with performance reviews.
Under this system salary, increments, bonuses and similar
incentives are awarded on the basis of a person's
performance.

Reward reviews can be a cost-effective method of
motivating employees by providing a monetary incentive to
effective performers. However, the assessments on which
rewards are based are usually subjective and reward reviews
can be divisive because the employees that do not receive
rewards may complain of favouritism and become
discouraged.

TRAINING AND DEVELOPING YOUR TEAM

The reward review is usually separate from the appraisal system but is often based on some of the information provided by performance appraisal. Reward systems will have a good chance of working if:

- they are introduced after consultation with managers, employees and trade unions
- the system is simple to understand
- managers are trained to carry out the reviews
- everybody has clear information on how the system will operate
- the appraisal and reward system are separate
- the system is closely monitored
- employees see and comment on their assessment ratings
- an appeals procedure is available.

Personal development planning

Some, particularly the larger, organizations have introduced a system of personal development planning. Each member of staff has their own personal development plan and meets with their line manager regularly, say six monthly, to discuss their work objectives and their development needs to support the achievement of their personal objectives. The regular reviews are used to check progress on personal development and to set new personal development targets. This type of system encourages the continuous development of everybody working in the organization and ensures that an individual's development needs are closely linked to work objectives.

Your responsibility to develop your team

We have looked at a number of methods that are used by organizations to review the performance of their staff. Very often the result of these reviews is that training and development needs are identified by you or a team member. The needs must be met for each individual within the team and so the team can perform more effectively. It is your responsibility to ensure that, as far as the budget allows, your team members are given the opportunities they need to fulfil their potential. It can be a complicated business arranging appropriate training and development for your team. It helps if you keep at the forefront of your mind that the short-term inconvenience it may cause is worth it for the long-term benefit that you and the team will gain.

Training is a means of transferring skills and knowledge. It is any learning activity which is directed towards the acquisition of specific knowledge and skills for the purpose of an occupation or task. Training is not the same as development; the focus of development is to prepare the individual for future needs, rather than present needs. Education is not the same as training or development; education is a long-term learning activity which meets the individual's specific needs, although education in the sense of working towards a professional management qualification is linked to training.

Staff need training for a variety of reasons:

• to learn how to do a new job
• to learn a new way of doing their job, for example, following the introduction of new technology
• to get rid of bad habits which have developed over time
• to develop the individual team member.

It is worth thinking about the differences between training, education and development. Education is a long-term learning activity, such as a management course, which will prepare the participant for a variety of roles. Training is a learning activity through which the individual acquires specific knowledge and skills to improve performance in their job role. Development is a learning activity that is designed to meet the future needs of the participant. It is concerned with growing into a new role and less concerned with improving performance now.

In this chapter we mainly deal with training as, in your role as a team leader, it is training with which you will be mostly involved.

As a team leader you have a major role to play in the development of your team. You not only need to establish who needs training and when, but you often have to select a suitable method of training; you probably spend much of your time training your team, in order to assist them to do their jobs more effectively.

It is certainly in your interests to take the training of your team seriously; you will improve current skills, increase the

TRAINING AND DEVELOPING YOUR TEAM

range of skills that members of your team can offer and develop future skills in your team. The major benefit is that training and development will lead to greater motivation within your team.

Many of you will work in large organizations, where training is not simply the responsibility of the team leader. Your organization might have a sophisticated training department and so it is essential that you work together with any partners involved in training to ensure that your team benefit from the correct training. It is important that your organization demonstrates a commitment to training and provides the necessary resources for training.

Your manager will probably make some decisions in consultation with you about the type of training that is suitable for staff, and you need to speak to your manager about appropriate training for your team. The trainee also has a responsibility for their own training; it is important that the trainee wants to learn and adopts the kind of attitude that means they will benefit from the training.

In some professions there are professional bodies which assist their members to develop and progress in their careers by maintaining professional standards through an examination structure and offering appropriate opportunities for continuing professional development.

In Chapter 8, 'Managing Yourself', we look at the different ways in which individuals learn. Try to identify the learning styles of your team so that you can select activities that 'fit' with their preferred learning style.

Types of training

When you are selecting a suitable training method you need to consider how the person that you wish to train prefers to learn (see Chapter 7 for an explanation of preferred learning styles), the cost of the training – both the actual costs and the hidden costs, for example, being away from the workplace – and the time that will need to be invested for the training to be effective.

On-the-job training

On the job training takes place in the normal workplace of the job holder, often using all the equipment that the trainee would normally use in the workplace. See

Figure 6.3 for an outline of the various types of on-the-job training.

The advantages of on-the-job training are that there is nothing like the real thing. As long as the trainee is carefully supervised, this type of training is very useful.

The problem with on-the-job training is that it is for real and any mistakes could cause serious problems.

Skill practice	Under the supervision of the trainer, the trainee performs the skill that the trainee is learning
Demonstration	The trainer shows the trainee exactly how to carry out the task
Projects	The trainee is given a particular project which has been chosen to enhance their knowledge and skills
Sitting with 'Nellie'	This is where a trainee is passed to an experienced member of the team who looks after the trainee and shows them the ropes
Coaching	This involves continuing informal advice and assistance, usually from the trainee's line manager
Mentoring	A mentor is a role model, tutor, coach and confidant within the organization who supports the learner
Delegation	Trainer delegates some of their own work to trainee
Secondment	Trainee is seconded to a new role for a period of time

Figure 6.3
On-the-job training

Activity 33

Complete the following table.

Type of training	Advantages	Problems
Skill practice		
Demonstration		
Projects		
Sitting with 'Nellie'		
Coaching		
Mentoring		
Delegation		
Secondment		

See Feedback section for answer to this activity.

There are two types of on-the-job training which have grown in popularity over the past few years and so are worth looking at in a little more detail.

Coaching

Coaching is on-the-job training which is supported by feedback on performance. It uses the work situation as a learning opportunity and relies on the coach spending time with the person being coached which helps the learner to develop continuously.

It is important that you develop coaching skills which will help you in your role as a first line manager. Coaching is not a systematic training activity, it is about spotting training opportunities as they arise in the workplace and using the opportunities to develop the skills and knowledge of the person being coached.

A good coach requires a number of skills: a coach needs to be able to listen, question, observe, evaluate and analyse information. In addition, the coach needs to encourage the learner, build confidence and give support.

Effective coaching

Sometimes coaching just happens, but it is most successful if the coach is skilled and the session has been prepared and is pre-planned. For effective coaching to take place, managers need to adopt a planned approach. The coach can do this by:

1 Identifying a learning requirement. The coach needs to:

- talk to the learner about their job and self-development needs
- watch the learner at work and notice areas in which performance could be improved
- look at the learner's work and establish strengths and weaknesses.

2 Plan and prepare to meet the learner's need. The coach needs to:

- identify the standard of performance required in a particular job
- identify appropriate coaching methods
- plan how to help the learner to achieve the appropriate standard.

3 Do the coaching. The coach needs to:

- conduct coaching sessions
- carry out reviews with the learner to find out how the learner is progressing
- allow the learner the time and access to the resources they need.

4 Evaluate the success of the coaching. The coach needs to:

- ask the learner for their view of the coaching programme
- establish if the coaching and development is achieving the objectives you have set
- establish if people are better at their jobs as a result of the coaching
- establish whether the costs of, and the disruption caused by, the coaching made the whole thing worthwhile.

Try to learn from your experience as a coach and try to improve your coaching as a result. Effective coaching is much more than just another method of implementing training. The advantages of coaching are:

- it occurs on the job and is cost effective
- it provides relevant learning, learning by doing and feedback on performance
- the learner will be adopting methods of learning that have your full support
- it develops the coach as well as the recipient of the coaching
- it can be done informally, without the learner recognizing that they are being coached or it can be formalized with regular review sessions for those people who prefer to be systematic
- it can be very motivating for people.

Mentoring

Another form of staff development that is increasing in popularity is the use of mentors. Mentoring is a way of developing individuals to reach their potential. Mentoring is when a senior 'expert' person within an organization 'adopts' an employee to develop their potential and to support their career development.

A mentor :

- gives encouragement and help to enable the learner to build confidence
- provides a role model on which a learner can base behaviour
- talks, listens and shares experiences
- does not tell the learner what to do
- arranges opportunities for the learner to do or try something new.

The role of the mentor is to:	and to encourage the learner to:
listen	listen
question, to elicit facts	clarify understanding
give information and knowledge about the organization, its politics and informal networks	share thinking
give advice on career development	review and reflect on own behaviour and experience
offer different perspectives	challenge own assumptions
offer support and encouragement	consider different perspectives
draw on own experience when appropriate	develop and manage a career plan
confront and discuss current issues	take responsibility for their own personal development and prepare for the next level of management
take the lead and make decisions – at least early in the relationship	make decisions for maximizing the outcomes of the mentor relationship

Figure 6.4 The role of the mentor and learner in the mentor relationship

TRAINING AND DEVELOPING YOUR TEAM

This type of mentoring relationship is valuable for both individuals and organizations because it is about achieving personal growth and development and not just about learning new skills or knowledge. The foundation of the relationship must be based on trust and respect. This requires a high degree of personal competence from the mentor. Mentoring is not a tutor/student relationship, nor an instructor/trainee relationship, nor a manager/employee relationship nor a friend/friend relationship. It is quite different.

Mentoring has the advantage of inducting newcomers efficiently to the organization and assisting them with organizational problems and personal development, thereby increasing motivation and job satisfaction. The mentor can also pass on organizational culture. Figure 6.4 shows the role of the mentor and learner in the mentor relationship.

Activity 34

Would you make a good mentor? Complete the checklist below to see how you measure up.

Do you have . . .?

- relevant job-related experience and skills ☐
- well-developed interpersonal skills ☐
- an ability to relate well to learners ☐
- a desire to help and develop learners ☐
- an open mind and a flexible attitude ☐
- a recognition of your own need for support ☐
- time to develop relationships with learners ☐

Would your team members make good learners? Do they have: . . .?

- a commitment to their own development ☐
- a flexible approach to new methods of learning ☐
- an honest and open attitude to their own behaviour ☐
- a willingness to accept feedback ☐
- time and willingness to develop a relationship with the mentor ☐

Mentoring has many advantages for all concerned. These are shown in Figure 6.5.

PEOPLE AND SELF MANAGEMENT

Advantages for the organization	Advantages for the mentor	Advantages for the learner
• helps to recruit staff	• job satisfaction	• improved confidence and self-esteem
• helps to develop and retain experienced staff	• peer recognition	• sense of value within the organization
• helps to develop and retain younger, less experienced staff	• development opportunity	• potential advancement and career opportunities
• invests in and develops own people	• career advancement	• 'safe' learning environment to cope with formal and informal structures of the organization, especially on recruitment but also ongoing and on-the-job
• provides an opportunity to discuss and promote learning throughout the organization		• help and support
• helps to disseminate the organization's values and develop its culture		
• improves communications		
• enhances the practice and culture of continuous improvement		

Figure 6.5 The advantages of mentoring

Off-the-job training

For this type of training, the trainee is taken away from the normal workplace, either to a special training area or to another organization. Figure 6.6 shows the main types of off-the-job training.

Advantages of off-the-job training are that the trainee can concentrate fully on the training, without any distractions. Any mistakes the trainee makes are not going to have serious consequences.

Disadvantages of off-the-job training are that the trainee is away from the workplace and their job needs to be covered by colleagues.

TRAINING AND DEVELOPING YOUR TEAM

Simulation	A simulated task is carried out by the trainee
Lectures and talks	The trainer delivers a prepared talk on an aspect of work, such as health and safety
Discussions	Group discussions, useful for generating ideas and solutions
College course	(a) Long college course, leads to a qualification and covers a wide range of skills and knowledge (b) Short college course, supplements in-company training
Internal training course	Designed and delivered by the organization for the organization, so will specifically meet organizational needs
Distance/open learning course	A course leading to qualifications can be undertaken without the disadvantage of releasing the employee from the workplace. The student can fit the study around their work and personal commitments
Consultants/ external trainers	Fill gaps in in-company provision, tailor-made to meet clients needs
Computer-based training	Trainee works through interactive computer packages that have been specially designed for training staff

Figure 6.6
Off-the-job training

The training gap and the training cycle

Training at work is required to fill what is known as the 'training gap'. The training gap is illustrated in Figure 6.7.

In order to establish exactly what the training gap is the team leader must have a clear idea about exactly what skills and knowledge are required to do all the jobs in the section and exactly what each team member can do. The training gap

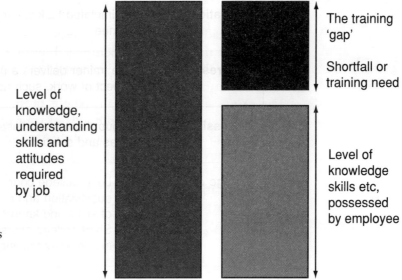

Figure 6.7
The training gap.
Reprinted by
permission of Bankers
Books. From
Supervisory Skills by
Sally Palmer (1996)

is the training need that each individual team member has.
You can fill the gap by organizing training to meet the need. If
you follow the training cycle shown in Figure 6.8 you will
ensure that your team is trained to carry out the necessary
tasks as effectively as possible.

Investigate 13

Does your organization have a training policy? If so, get a
copy and read through it. How is training arranged in your
organization? Does your organization have a training
department?

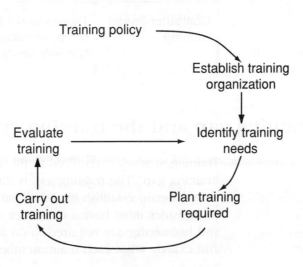

Figure 6.8
The training cycle

Identification and analysis of training needs

We already know that an appraisal system indicates the training needs of team members, but their are many other triggers that may indicate a training need. Some examples are given in Figure 6.9.

You can also conduct an analysis of the job description and person specification for the jobs of your team members and then identify what skills the job holder already has and any skills they do not have which they need to do the job. This kind of analysis will enable you to produce a training specification for the individual.

When you have identified what the training needs of your team are, write down the objectives of the training. If you are clear what you want to get out of the training you will be able

Change

- new legislation
- new technology
- new markets
- new products
- new methods of working.

Information

Some information that is available to you might indicate that you should be thinking about training your team, for example:

- customer complaints
- high turnover of staff
- quality of work
- poor work rate, i.e. output
- conflict within the team
- demotivated team.

Automatic

Some situations automatically indicate that training is required, for example:

- new starters – induction
- transfers in to the office
- promotion
- appraisal.

Figure 6.9
Triggers indicating a training need

to evaluate the training and check whether or not the objectives have been achieved. The objectives should be exact statements about what the trainee should be able to do at the end of the training.

It will help to draw up a training matrix similar to the one shown in Figure 6.10. Each task is an aspect of the work of the section. This provides you with a simple chart showing who can do what and enables you to see at a glance what training is required for all your team members to acquire the skills they need.

You can see from the matrix that some members of the team are more multi-skilled than others. You need to decide how many staff you require to carry out each task and who is capable of developing further. It is a good idea to discuss the matrix and your plans with your team.

Activity 35

Construct a training matrix for the team that you supervise or are a member of.

Tasks	Susan	Jane	Fred	Abdul	Pat
Prepare all types of surface for painting	✓	✓		✓	✓
Undercoat all types of surface	✓			✓	✓
Topcoat all types of surface	✓	✓	✓		
Prepare walls for paper hanging			✓	✓	✓
Hang paper – simple patterns			✓		✓
Hang paper – complex patterns			✓		✓
and so on . . .					

Figure 6.10 Training matrix – Painting and decorating section

TRAINING AND DEVELOPING YOUR TEAM

Planning training

Once you have established what training is required by the team, you can draw up a training plan. Differentiate between the training priorities. What needs immediate action? What training can you arrange? What training must you discuss with your manager? The training plan should cover:

- what training is to be provided
- how it is to be provided
- when it is to be provided
- by whom it is to be provided
- where it is to be provided
- at what cost it is to be provided.

You will probably have a training manual at work in which all the available training courses in your organization are detailed. These types of manuals usually give the following details:

- title of course
- level of course
- training objectives
- content
- details of any pre-training requirements
- details of any post-training requirements.

This type of manual is useful for you to refer to, as it enables you to establish exactly what is available.

Activity 36

Choose a training programme you have been involved with, either as a learner or as a trainer.

List the objectives of the training.

What methods were used for checking that the training objectives had been met?

Evaluate whether the training objectives were met.

Bearing in mind your evaluation, what changes would you like to make to the training programme?

Carry out training

Implement your training plans. Do what you have planned to do.

Evaluate the training

Whatever method of training you use remember to give the trainee feedback, to let them know how they have performed. Do not criticise, give helpful constructive feedback; remember, feedback is to help people change their behaviour in a positive way. Remember to praise.

When one of your team returns from a training course make sure that you debrief them so that you can discuss the training course with them and plan how they will practise their new skills and knowledge in the workplace. If the training course has not met the individual's or your expectations, contact the training department and tell them what the problem is.

Evaluate the training. Has the training met the objectives? Honest evaluation will help you to evaluate progress and train, or organize the training, better next time.

Investigate 14

How is training evaluated in your organization?

The benefits of training

There are many benefits of training, both to the organization and to the employee.

Benefits to the organization:

* staff will have appropriate skills
* improved job performance and productivity
* improved service quality
* increased motivation.

Benefits to the individual:

* increased self-confidence
* improved range and quality of skills
* improved job satisfaction
* improved prospects of promotion within the organization
* better chance of obtaining a job outside the organization.

TRAINING AND DEVELOPING YOUR TEAM

Summary   We have covered appraisal in this chapter and noted how the appraiser usually indicates that the appraisee has training needs. We have covered the many different types of training available and looked at how to identify training needs, plan and evaluate training. Training and developing your team will lead to higher levels of performance, better quality of work and a more highly motivated team. Appraising, training and developing your team are crucial aspects of a team leader's role.

Review and discussion questions

1 What are the purposes of appraisal?
2 What are the features and benefits of a good appraisal system?
3 What are the potential problems with appraisal?
4 What is the aim of the appraisal interview?
5 What questions does the appraisee need to know the answer to by the end of the appraisal interview?
6 What should the appraisee do to prepare for the appraisal interview?
7 What is meant by the term 'reward review'?
8 Why do staff need training?
9 What is the team leader's role in training?
10 What is meant by the term 'training gap'?
11 List ten training triggers.
12 What are the advantages and disadvantages of both on-the-job and off-the-job training?
13 How do you establish the training needs for your section?
14 What six key factors should a training plan cover?
15 How effective is your organization's appraisal system in achieving its objectives?
16 If you were given the power to implement one single improvement to your organization's appraisal system, what would you suggest and why?
17 Describe the objectives and the content of any training course you have attended in your work place. Give your opinion as to whether the course achieved its objectives. What are your reasons for considering it a success or failure?
18 What are the team leader's responsibilities towards a staff member who is about to go on a course at a training centre: before, during and after the course?

19 What topics would you include on a two-day training course called 'The new team leader'. What are your reasons for including each topic?

20 Think of a member of your team with a training need. How would you define exactly what the need is and how can you meet the need?

Case study

You have recently been appointed as a team leader in your organization. You have a team of ten staff with a wide range of experience. Unfortunately your predecessor, who has recently retired, did not keep any training records at all: he had worked for the organization for many years and knew what everybody could do, but unfortunately for you he kept all this information in his head. How will you go about setting up a system in your department for finding out exactly who can do what tasks and whether or not your team members have any training needs?

Work-based assignment

Carry out an analysis of one of your team member's developmental needs. Using the headings given below, produce a report explaining how you established the training needs, how you planned for the training, arranged for the training to be carried out and how you evaluated the training.

1 A brief overview of the team member's job role.
2 The objectives of the team member's job.
3 Establishing the training needs.
4 Planning the training required.
5 Carrying out the training.
6 Evaluating the training.
7 What I have learnt from doing this work-based assignment.

TRAINING AND DEVELOPING YOUR TEAM

7 Assessing and developing your own performance

Learning objectives

At the end of this chapter you will be able to:

- appreciate the need for self development
- understand the different ways in which people learn
- describe the learning cycle
- conduct a personal audit
- set self-development objectives
- identify development needs
- devise a self-development plan
- record and monitor progress against the self-development plan.

Introduction

The rate of change has become so rapid that if any person in work is to simply keep up with what is happening around them and to know enough to do their job effectively, it is essential for them to constantly update their skills and knowledge. These days it is widely accepted that education and training is a lifelong process and we have to develop new skills, acquire new knowledge and continuously update our methods of working if we are to be successful at work, and if British business is to be competitive in world markets. The government actively supports the 'lifelong learning' concept by national initiatives such as 'Investors in People' and 'Learning Accounts'. Many professional bodies encourage their members to keep records of their continuing self development. Some make continuing self development, under the title 'continuing professional development' (or CPD), compulsory.

Self development

Self development, or personal development, is about developing your own skills and knowledge so that you are continuously learning and developing yourself. If you are to be committed to your self development you need to take ownership of it by following the guidelines below:

- you become a learner
- you take responsibility for your own learning
- you establish your own needs for your development for personal growth and improved work performance
- you use a range of flexible learning methods, formal and informal, as methods of self development (learning is not always about 'going on a training course')
- you learn how you learn best and use this information as you commit to your own continuous self development.

Activity 37	List the benefits that you and your organization will gain if you make a commitment to your own self development.

See Feedback section for answer to this activity.

How people learn

In order to understand what type of training and development is appropriate for you, you need to know something about how people learn. You need this information to enable you to think more clearly about what type of learning will suit you best. Learning can be defined as 'acquiring knowledge of, or skill in, by study, experience, or instruction'. There are various types of learning that take place throughout our working life:

- *intuitive* – this is the more or less automatic response to new information or activities; learning takes place without you being aware that it is happening
- *incidental* – this is when a particular event happens, and it makes you think about what happened and why it happened; this type of learning is more conscious
- *retrospective* – this type of learning takes place when you systematically make a habit of thinking about activities and events and analysing what you learnt from them

ASSESSING AND DEVELOPING YOUR OWN PERFORMANCE

- *prospective* – this is the most active method of learning, this is when you plan to learn before an experience and then review the learning experience afterwards. This is the most effective and powerful type of learning. If you are serious about your own self development you ought to be constantly involved in prospective learning.

The learning cycle

The learning cycle is shown in Figure 7.1. The learning cycle shows that effective learning consists of four linked stages:

1 having the experience
2 reviewing the experience – thinking about this particular experience, what happened and why it happened
3 concluding from the experience – deciding how valid and relevant the learning has been
4 trying it out and planning the next steps.

To gain the most benefit from self development, you need consciously to go through the whole of the learning cycle.

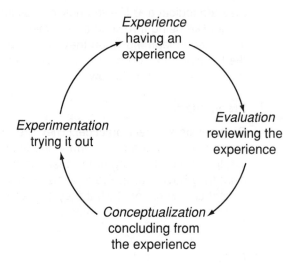

Figure 7.1
The learning cycle

Learning styles

There has been a good deal of research done on how adults learn. David Kolb, Alan Mumford and Peter Honey, in particular, have suggested that there are four main learning styles. These are shown in Figure 7.2.

Activists

Activists like to be involved in new experiences. They like to solve new problems and to be involved in new opportunities. They like the excitement of change and working in a team. Activists enjoy high visibility roles, such as chairing meetings, leading discussions and giving presentations. They do not like learning by watching and prefer not to learn by reading or in any passive way.

Reflectors

Reflectors like to think carefully and like time to think things through before taking any action. They are inquisitive but measured; they learn best from watching and carrying out research themselves. Reflectors do not like to be the centre of attention or being rushed; they learn less from situations where they do not have time to be as thorough as usual.

Theorists

Theorists learn best when they have an opportunity to methodically explore the linkages between situations, events and ideas. They are comfortable with concepts and theories; they are logical and like to question assumptions. Theorists do not like being thrown in at the deep end and are only interested in learning when they can clearly see the value of the learning; they do not like to be involved in things that they perceive to be shallow.

Pragmatists

Pragmatists are very practical. They like to see, very clearly, the link between learning and the job they are doing. They like to put their learning to the test and try out and implement what they have learnt. Pragmatists do not learn well if they cannot clearly connect what they are learning to their work, to a specific problem that they are dealing with.

Figure 7.2
Dominant learning styles

ASSESSING AND DEVELOPING YOUR OWN PERFORMANCE

An important development of Kolb's work is the 'Learning Style Questionnaire'. The object of the questionnaire is to help individuals to identify their learning style, i.e. the way they go about solving problems. The results of the test can be logged on to a chart and the individual's dominant learning style is established.

It is easier for you to seek out the type of learning experiences that suit your particular style. It also enables you to be aware of the type of learning which does not suit your style and to try to overcome any mental blocks that you have to a particular type of learning experience. A good team leader will also know the type of learning which suits members of their own team, in order to set up the most productive training programme for them.

Activity 38

It is important that you identify your current preferred learning style. Establish your own learning style by completing the activity below.

1 Review three past experiences and decide on the type of events from which you learnt most.

2 Completing a Learning Style Questionnaire.

3 Asking for the views of colleagues, friends and family.

You can now make an assessment of your own preferred learning style. Are your an Activist, Reflector, Theorist or Pragmatist?

Now you know what your preferred learning style is, you can identify ways in which you can improve your attitude to learning.

PEOPLE AND SELF MANAGEMENT

The stages of self development

There are four key steps that you need to carry out to set up a system for your self development:

1 *personal audit* – undertake an audit of where you are now, in terms of what you can do now

2 *setting self development objectives* – setting aims and objectives in terms of what you want to achieve. These will be both work-related and personal goals

3 *identifying development needs* – identifying the knowledge and skills that you will need to achieve your goals

4 *constructing the development plan* – analysing the information that has been revealed in 1 and 3 above, identifying the gaps. The gaps will form the basis of your development plan. Your self-development plan will motivate you to carry out your development, provide a tool to monitor and evaluate your achievements and provide a schedule to work to.

See Figure 7.3 for the self-development cycle.

It is a good idea to start a self-development file, a ring binder in which you can keep all your self-development

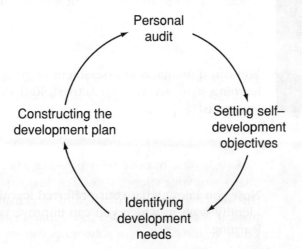

Figure 7.3
The self-development cycle

records; we will refer to this as your self-development portfolio. Your contents list might look like this:

SELF-DEVELOPMENT PORTFOLIO

Contents list

Section 1 Personal audit
An analysis of my preferred learning style
Curriculum vitae
Training courses I have attended
Personal SWOT analysis

Section 2 Self-development objectives
Section 3 Self-development plan
Section 4 Self-development reviews

We will now look at each of these stages in more detail.

Undertaking a personal audit

The personal audit involves assessing your current level of knowledge and listing your current skills and abilities. There are various tools that you can use to inform your personal audit. Enlist the support of your line manager and others with whom you work.

A good place to start is with your current CV, this will have the information about your previous job experience and any qualifications that you have.

Activity 39

Update your CV and put a copy in your new self-development file.

Activity 40

Produce a list of all the training courses that you have undertaken in the last five years. Place this in your self-development portfolio.

Now it is time to conduct a personal SWOT analysis, i.e. an analysis of your strengths, weaknesses, opportunities and threats. This is a good method of establishing where you are now. It is also a good idea to ask one or more people you know well to complete a swot on you.

| Activity 41 | Complete the following SWOT analysis. Put the results in your self-development portfolio. |

Strengths		Weaknesses	
Prompt	Comment	Prompt	Comment
Qualifications		Gaps in my qualifications	
Work experience		Gaps in my work experience	
Knowledge		Gaps in my knowledge	
Skills		Gaps in my skills	
Money and resources		Financial pressures	
Support from family		Problems in my personal circumstances	
Support from my colleagues		Enemies at work	
Health		Health	
The circumstances in which I have felt most happy and fulfilled		The circumstances in which I have felt most unhappy and frustrated	
Strong points of character and personality		Weak points of character and personality	
Contacts		Contacts	
Motivation and drive		What has held me back in achieving my objectives?	
Any other strengths		Any other limitations	

Now complete your own analysis of opportunities and threats.

Opportunities	Threats
1	1
2	2
3	3
4	4
5	5
6	6
7	7
8	8
9	9
10	10

Things I am particularly proud of:

```
1
2
3
4
5
```

Things I am particularly disappointed about:

```
1
2
3
4
5
```

What does the result of your self analysis tell you about yourself?

> The results of my self analysis tell me:

When you have completed the analysis take plenty of time to evaluate the result. Do not allow your weaknesses to demotivate and discourage you. Use them to spur you into action to do something about them.

Setting self-development objectives

Now you are ready to clarify your personal objectives. These are the types of questions you need to ask yourself:

- Where do I want to be in the future in the short and the long term?
- Will I remain a team leader forever?
- Do I want to continue to work for the same organization?
- Do I need to update my skills in the light of new technology?
- Do I need to learn new management techniques?
- Do I need to develop any personal skills?
- Do I have the right balance between work and home life?
- Do I spend enough time on my favourite leisure pursuits?
- Is there anything I have always wanted to do and not done? If so why haven't I done it?
- Do I need to undertake any further education?

For each of the gaps you have identified, set yourself development objectives. Your development objectives need to be SMART like all objectives:

- Specific
- Measurable
- Achievable
- Realistic
- Timely

ASSESSING AND DEVELOPING YOUR OWN PERFORMANCE

My personal objectives

Area for objectives	Detailed objective
Education	
Career	
Interests	
Leisure	
Social	

Identifying your own development needs

Your development will encompass a wide range of learning activities which can take place over the short and the long term. Your development should take place through a series of planned experiences. The following list gives examples of the types of development activities you might use to meet your development needs.

- workplace experience and practice
- action learning/special assignments
- peer group contacts
- reading
- work shadowing
- coaching and tutoring
- mentoring
- delegation
- distance learning
- job rotation
- secondment
- job enrichment
- counselling
- community involvement.

Your self-development plan

Now you have completed your personal audit, set your objectives and identified your development needs, you need to write your self-development plan. This is your action plan which will show how you intend to fill the gaps that you have identified, and when you will review your progress. If there are no gaps, it is unlikely that your analysis has been done properly; it is unlikely that you would be so knowledgeable, skilled and perfect that you have no development needs at all!

As shown in Figure 7.4, your self-development plan shows how you will carry out the development process.

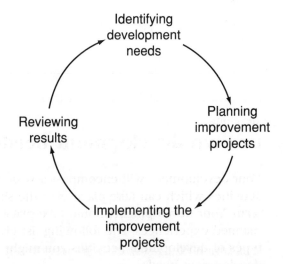

Figure 7.4
The self-development process

Constructing your self-development plan

The way to work out how you are going to fill your self-development gap and meet your self-development needs is to list your needs and match them with the most effective form of learning that will meet each need.

Your development plan needs to show your development objectives, what you intend to do to meet your development needs and when you will review your progress against your plans. Ideally your development plan should include a range of learning activities which suit your learning style, and include a balance of both formal and informal learning experiences. See the example in Figure 7.5.

ASSESSING AND DEVELOPING YOUR OWN PERFORMANCE

Development objectives	Proposed action				
	Proposed development	Date development undertaken	Review date	Outcomes of development activity and review comments	Further action
1					
2					
3					
4					
5					

Figure 7.5 Example of a development plan

10.2 Barriers to self development

It is difficult for many of us to actually get down to constructing our self-development plan. There are many reasons we might give for not involving ourselves in structured self development, such as:

- I haven't got time
- I've managed without it so far
- I need someone to organize it for me
- I'm too old to change my ways now.

Do any of these barriers apply to you? If so, it is time for you to rethink your attitude to self development. It is important to find the time that you need for your self development; you may have managed so far, but it is going to be increasingly difficult to manage in the future. Only *you* can manage *your* self development and you are never too old to change your ways - if you want to!

Planning the support you need for your self development

You will find it useful to identify the people who can help you achieve your self-development objectives. It is your responsibility to ask for help when you need it. There is no doubt that you will find it useful to have a mentor within your workplace to provide essential support. We looked at the role of a mentor in Chapter 6 and so you already know the contribution that a mentor can make to the achievement of your self-development objectives. There will also be contacts both within your organization and outside your organization, who will be able to help you, such as:

- colleagues and managers at work – such as your line manager or personnel manager
- friends and acquaintances outside work – personal contacts who may have particular skills and experience and could help you with your personal and career development.

You can probably think of other types of contacts that may provide you with support, such as community groups.

Activity 42

Now you are ready to complete your own self-development plan.

Recording your progress

It is a good idea to keep an up-to-date record of your personal learning; you can use this information to regularly update your self-development plan. This type of record also makes life much easier when you need to update your CV and/or if you belong to a professional body which requires you to keep a record of your CPD. An example of such a record is shown below.

Date	Description of the event	What I learnt from the event	How I will use the learning

ASSESSING AND DEVELOPING YOUR OWN PERFORMANCE

At least once a year conduct a thorough review of your plan. Re-assess your goals honestly and ensure that they are still valid. Revisit your learning objectives and update them.

Summary

In this chapter we have looked at the importance of self development and you have a set of practical tools you can use to establish, in a structured way, exactly what your development needs are. Hopefully you will be motivated enough to maintain a CPD portfolio – I do and I can assure you that it is very constructive and useful to put time aside to concentrate on your development needs. If you do not, nobody else will!

Review and discussion questions

1 What benefits will you and your organization gain, if you maintain a self-development portfolio?
2 List the four types of learning that take place throughout your working life.
3 Draw the learning cycle.
4 Briefly describe the four main learning styles described by Peter Honey.
5 List the four key steps that you need to carry out to set up a system for your self development.
6 What should the four sections of your self-development portfolio be entitled?
7 Why is it important to set self-development objectives?
8 Objectives have to be SMART, what does this mean?
9 List four common barriers to self development.
10 How often should you re-assess your self-development goals?

Case study Steve is a team leader. He is 35 years old and has four children aged 10, 6, 4 and 2. He is a keen cyclist and spends most Sundays pursuing his hobby. He leads his team well. He is very keen on keeping them motivated and providing them with opportunities to develop themselves. He is hard working and ensures that all his team members keep up-to-date. The team have all recently been trained to use the new computer software that has been installed and Steve ensures that they all receive regular technical updating. Steve was booked to go on a computer course himself, but one of the team was off sick and he thought it might create problems if he went on the course, so he cancelled. The only person who has not undertaken any development activities in the last three years is Steve. Is Steve taking a risk by ignoring his own development needs? What advice would you give Steve?

Work-based assignment

C1.1

Construct and complete your personal development portfolio.

8 Managing yourself

Learning objectives

On completion of this chapter you will be able to:

- list the essential requirements for good time management
- identify time wasters
- explain techniques for managing time more effectively
- manage your own time more effectively
- differentiate between submissive, aggressive and assertive behaviour
- describe your assertive rights
- behave assertively
- explain the advantages of assertive behaviour
- understand the causes of stress
- utilize coping strategies to deal with stress.

Introduction

So far we have looked at various aspects of management which have all been concerned with managing other people. If you are to be an effective manager, one of the most important things you must learn is how to manage yourself effectively. In the last chapter we looked at analysing yourself so that you could establish what you need to do, to continue to develop yourself and so become a better manager. In this chapter we will look at the essential skill of managing yourself.

Time management

One essential attribute every good manager should have is the ability to use their time effectively. Remember, time will always fly by; it is your effective use of that time which reflects upon your effectiveness as a manager. Effective managers are able to organize themselves and organize other people. To do this, you must plan how you use your time.

Keep in the forefront of your mind the purpose of your job. Ask yourself – what am I here for? Always ensure that you are spending your time in a way that is relevant to your job.

There are a number of procedures and techniques for time management, some of which we will examine now. Four key essential requirements for good time management are:

1 clear objectives
2 forward planning
3 the ability to prioritize and focus on action
4 the ability to delegate successfully.

Time wasters

Everyone wastes time. Defining exactly what is a time waster is quite difficult. A very general definition of a time waster is any activity that takes time unnecessarily or uses time inappropriately. Common time wasters are listed in Figure 8.1.

You need to be aware of what your time wasters are, determine and deal with the root cause.

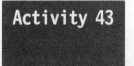
Activity 43

See Figure 8.2 for a sample time log. Keep a time log at work for a week, recording how you spend your time each day. The log will have to be quite detailed. You can use the information gleaned to identify your time wasters and then, do something about them!

Techniques for managing time more effectively

1 Treat time as your most valuable resource.

2 Identify and regularly review your own objectives.

Clarify the purpose of your job. Ask yourself:

• what am I here for?
• what are my objectives?

Your objectives will relate to the objectives of your department and organization.

MANAGING YOURSELF

TIME WASTERS	
Meetings	Irrelevant meetings, meetings without an agenda, meetings without an end time
Inability to say no	Feeling that you have to be all things to all people, never saying no
Poor communication	Your own communication and others
Telephone calls	Unnecessarily lengthy discussions
Drop-ins	'I was just passing and dropped in for a chat. Did you know ...? Have you heard ...?'
Bosses	'I need this now. Can you get me this immediately? You'll have to drop everything for this one'
Unclear goals	Uncertainty about what you are doing. Constantly seeking clarification
Conflicting priorities	Too many bosses? Too many tasks?
Waiting for others' work	Inefficient teams. Unclear goals?
Poor delegation	Your inability to delegate
Incompetent staff	Badly trained teams?
Too much work	Simply too much to do!
Attempting to do too much	Taking on more than your fair share
Procrastination	Putting off tasks we do not like

Figure 8.1 Common time wasters. Reprinted by permission of Bankers Books. From *Supervisory Skills* by Sally Palmer (1996)

Time log			
Time	**Task**	**Interruptions**	
		Phone	**Person**
8.30			
8.45			
9.00			
9.15			
9.30			
9.45			
10.00			
10.15			
10.30			
10.45			
11.00			
11.15			
11.30			
11.45			
12.00			
12.15			
12.30			
12.45			
1.00			
1.15			
1.30			
1.45			
2.00			
2.15			
2.30			
2.45			
3.00			
3.15			
3.30			
3.45			
4.00			
4.15			
4.30			
4.45			
5.00			
5.15			
5.30			
5.45			
6.00			

Figure 8.2 Time log

3 Research the present use of time.

Keep a careful and regular record of how you spend your time over at least a week. Analyse it looking for:

- time under your own control
- time spent reacting to others.

Aim at taking control of at least 50 per cent of your time. Mark or note periods of wasted time by self or others. Discard pointless activity. Monitor and control the use of time on a continuous basis.

4 Develop a sound system for allocating priorities.

Tasks usually fall into two categories:

- positive active tasks – working towards achieving the organizational objectives
- reactive tasks – daily running and maintenance needs.

To prioritize and schedule your work you need to know:

- how important the task is
- how urgent the task is.

Understand the difference between *important* and *urgent*.

- *Importance* decides how much effort and time you put into a task
- *urgency* dictates when you do it.

For example:

- if a task is urgent but unimportant then do it now but spend little time on it
- if a task is urgent and important then do it now and make sure that you spend sufficient time on it.

See Figure 8.3.

You can then prioritize the tasks you do in a 'things to do list'.

- A, must do today
- B, should do today but could do tomorrow
- C, should do this week.

Write a list of jobs you have got to get done, not just today's jobs but long-term tasks and priorities.

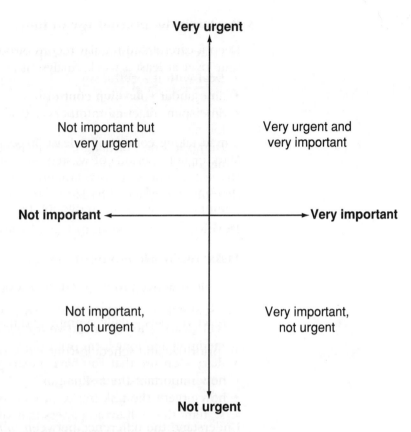

Figure 8.3
Urgent/important grid

5 Plan each day carefully.

Produce task lists each day, allocating priorities carefully using a 'to do list'.

6 Plan activities carefully.

Tackle large tasks by dividing them into smaller, more manageable, parts.

7 Allocate time for thinking.

8 Use assertiveness to prevent others from wasting your time.

Learn to say 'no', graciously but assertively.

9 Delegate everything you possibly can.

10 Deal with paperwork only <u>once</u>.

Use the four D's approach to paperwork:

- *D*eal with it – ruthlessly
- *D*elegate it – develop your staff
- *D*iarize it – if you are unable to deal with it today, mark forward
- *D*ump it – do not hang on to it. No bottom drawer. No pending.

Always have a tidy desk. Only have one pile of work to be completed. Always finish one job before you go on to the next.

11 Make use of time planning tools.

Use the following tools to cut down on time wasting:

- visual planners – such as wall chart year planner. This will clearly show you and your colleagues, your short-, medium- and long-term priorities
- diary – ensure that you have a diary that suits your needs and mark everything in it
- office diary system – make proper use of the office system, this will avoid papers that you are unable to deal with yet, lying around on your desk.

Assertive behaviour

Assertive rights are based on the fundamental notion that each individual adult is the ultimate judge of his or her own behaviour. It is about taking personal responsibility for your own actions.

How do you behave when people:

- criticize you
- shout at you, blame you for something you have not done
- keep you waiting
- interrupt you
- exploit you?

If you react defensively, you are being *submissive*.
If you attack, you are being *aggressive*.
The most satisfactory way to behave is to be *assertive*.

We will examine assertive behaviour in this chapter.

The difference between assertive, aggressive and submissive behaviour

Assertiveness is:

- recognizing your needs and asking openly and directly for what you want
- recognizing and respecting the needs of other people
- relating to people in personal and working situations in an open and honest way
- feeling responsible for, and in control of, our own actions
- not seeing situations in terms of win or lose, but being prepared to compromise
- being able to resolve difficulties and disputes in a way that feels comfortable and just to those involved.

Aggressiveness is:

- expressing feelings and opinions in a way that punishes, threatens or puts the other person down
- disregarding the rights and needs of others
- aiming to get your own way, no matter what
- if we 'win' and get what we want aggressively it probably leaves someone else with bad feelings, making it difficult to relate to them in the future.

Submissiveness is:

- not standing up for your rights
- allowing others to take advantage of you
- avoiding responsibility for making choices – leaving others to make decisions for you
- not being in control of your life
- seeing yourself as a helpless victim of unfairness or injustice
- being unable to ask for what you want.

Suppose you are asked to work late one Wednesday evening. You are already committed that evening and you are feeling over-stretched and over-worked anyway. You might reply in the following ways:

Submissive response	Aggressive response	Assertive response
Well, I don't really have the time, um er, I suppose that I could re-organize things to fit it in. I expect, er . . . well OK, I don't mind.	You have got to be joking! I'm up to my eyes in it already, anyway I'm doing something on Wednesday night. You'll have to find some other mug to do it.	I quite understand that it is important that somebody works late on Wednesday night. I can't help with that, however if I can assist in another way with the extra workload, I would be happy to discuss it with you.

Activity 44

Complete the last column of this chart.

Situation	Response	Assertive, aggressive or submissive?
1 A colleague interrupts you when you are making an important phone call.	'I'd like to finish this call, then I'll be happy to have a word with you.'	
2 Your partner asks you sarcastically what went wrong with the dinner preparations. (Dinner is not ready, as planned)	'If you expect me to be at your beck and call, you'd better think again. Get your own dinner.'	
3 Your boss praises the way you handled an awkward customer.	'It was nothing really. Sharon did all the hard work, I just came in at the end.'	

See Feedback section for answer to this activity.

Assertiveness is not just evident in what people say but also in how they behave. See Figure 8.4.

	Submissive	Aggressive	Assertive
Voice	• sometimes wobbly • tone may be singsong or whining • over-soft or over-warm • often dull and in monotone • quiet, often drops away at end.	• very firm • tone is sarcastic sometimes cold • hard and sharp • strident, often shouting, rises at end.	• steady and firm • tone is middle range and warm • sincere and clear • not too loud or quiet.
Speech pattern	• hesitant and filled with pauses • sometimes jerks from fast to slow • frequent throat-clearing.	• fluent, few awkward hesitances • often abrupt, clipped • emphazises blaming words • often fast.	• fluent, few awkward hesitances • emphasizes key words • steady, even pace.
Facial expression	• unreal smile when expressing anger, or being criticized • eyebrows raised in anticipation (e.g. of rebuke) • quick-changing features.	• smile may become 'wry' • scowls when angry • eyebrows raised in amazement/disbelief • jaw set firm • chin thrust forward.	• smiles when pleased • frowns when angry • otherwise 'open' • features steady, not wobbling • jaw relaxed but not 'loose'.
Eye contact	• evasive • looking-down.	• tries to stare down and dominate.	• firm but not a 'stare-down'.
Body movements	• hand-wringing • hunching shoulders • stepping back • covering mouth with hand • nervous movements which detract (shrugs and shuffles) • arms crossed for protection	• finger pointing • fist thimping • sits upright head 'in air' • stands upright head 'in air' • strides around (impatiently) • arms crossed (unapproachable).	• open hand movements (inviting to speak) • 'measured pace' hand movements • sits upright or relaxed (not slouching or cowering) • stands with head held straight.

Figure 8.4 Non-verbal aspects of submissive, aggressive and assertive behaviour

MANAGING YOURSELF

No one behaves assertively, aggressively or submissively all the time. You will vary your behaviour between all three. People are generally more likely to react aggressively or submissively, rather than assertively, in a conflict situation. Your reaction in a conflict situation is to do with your level of self-esteem. If you have low self-esteem, when conflict arises you will feel threatened and will tend to hit out (aggression) or be defensive (submission). You need to consider your rights. Learn to behave assertively and your self-esteem will improve.

Your rights

These assertive rights imply respect for yourselves and other people:

1. I have the right to be treated with respect as an intelligent, capable and equal human being
2. I have the right to state my own needs and set my own priorities as a person independent of any roles that I may assume in my life
3. I have the right to express my opinions and values
4. I have the right to say 'no' and 'yes' for myself
5. I have the right to make mistakes
6. I have the right to change my mind
7. I have the right to say 'I don't understand' and ask for more information
8. I have the right to ask for what I want
9. I have the right not to take responsibility for other people's problems
10. I have the right to deal with others without being dependent on them for approval.

Assertiveness skills

Be specific	Decide what you want or feel and say so specifically or directly. This skill helps you to be clear about exactly what it is you want to say. Avoid unnecessary padding and keep your statement simple and brief
Broken record (repetition)	Use calm repetition, over and over again. Using this technique, you can maintain a steady position. Keep repeating, for example, that it is not possible, that you do not agree
Fogging (fielding the response)	You need to indicate that you have heard what the other person said, without getting hooked on what they say. This skill allows you to acknowledge the response and still continue confidently with your statement
Workable compromise	Assertiveness is not about winning so you need to negotiate from an equal position. This means finding a true compromise which takes both parties' needs into consideration. Compromising on a solution to a difficult situation need not compromise your self-respect
Self disclosure	This skill allows you to disclose your feeling with a simple statement, for example, 'I feel nervous' or 'I feel guilty'. The effect is to reduce your anxiety, enabling you to relax and take charge of yourself and your feelings

Advantages of assertive behaviour

- *Close working relationships* – assertion tends to breed assertion, so people work more happily as a team. The team is then more likely to achieve its objectives.
- *Greater confidence in yourself* – you develop a stronger regard for yourself and a high level of self-esteem.

MANAGING YOURSELF

- *Greater confidence in others* – you will develop a healthy recognition of the capabilities and limitations of others – but not see them as inferior or superior.
- *Increased self responsibility* – you will take responsibility for yourself, your needs, wants and opinions rather than blaming others or excusing yourself.
- *Increased self control* – you will channel your thoughts and feelings to produce the behaviour you want, rather than being controlled by outside events, people or inner emotions.
- *Savings in time and energy* – you will take decisions more quickly based on their individual merit and save time when handling disputes. Much time and energy are wasted on worrying and scheming.

Managing stress

Most people get stressed from time to time. Stress is usually caused by external situations so it is not possible to remove stress totally. The key is learning how to cope with it.

Stress is not the same as pressure. Many people like pressure, it helps them to make an extra effort; it is exciting, challenging, energizing. It can make you feel stretched, valued and can encourage creativity. It is when pressure develops into stress that you start to experience problems.

Stress can make people very unhappy and cause physical illness together with poor performance at work. We need to be able to recognize the symptoms of stress so that we can take action and do something about it. Some symptoms are listed below:

- tiredness, caused by overwork, or difficulty sleeping
- rapid mood swings
- being irritable
- making mistakes at work
- fidgeting
- displacement activity – tidying out your desk when you have a pile of important work to do
- smoking/eating and drinking more than usual
- taking time off work
- withdrawing from your friends, colleagues and family.

PEOPLE AND SELF MANAGEMENT

It is also possible to display physical symptoms, such as:

- eating problems
- palpitations
- raised blood pressure
- sleep disorders
- nausea
- headaches
- back pain
- shoulder and neck pain.

This list is not exhaustive, but it gives some indication of the types of physical symptoms stress can induce.

If you know that you are suffering from stress, you can do something about it. The first thing to do is to try to establish what the cause of the stress is. There has been a great deal of research on the causes of stress. The types of things that cause stress are listed below.

Home-related stress	Work-related stress
Bereavement	Being dismissed or resigning
Divorce or separation	Being demoted
Illness	Financial problems for the self-employed
Financial worries	Problems with your boss
Becoming pregnant	Travelling to work
Giving birth	Failure to meet work objectives
Moving house	Missing deadlines
Major purchase	Feeling responsible for something going wrong at work
Retirement	Changing hours of work

There are, of course, many other causes of stress. The above lists merely give an indication of the types of things that cause people problems that can lead to stress.

There are actions that you can take to cope with stress:

1 you can remove the cause of the stress. This may be something simple such as taking the train to get to work, instead of driving. But sometimes it can be very difficult to remove the cause of stress, it might be easier to:

2 use coping techniques to help deal with the stress, such as:

- spending time on a hobby, such as swimming or reading
- do breathing and muscle exercises designed to relieve stress
- avoid caffeine
- try not to drink and smoke as much
- eat a balanced diet
- manage your time effectively
- get the right balance between home and work life
- spend some time each day doing nothing, even if it is only a few minutes.

If you follow the guidelines in the earlier part of this chapter, regarding managing your time and assertive behaviour, you will find these strategies help with the problems of stress.

Activity 45

Do you suffer from stress? Identify the reasons why and produce an action plan showing what you are going to do to alleviate the stress you are suffering from.

Summary

Now that you have read this chapter, you will appreciate the importance of good time management, you can identify your time wasters, and can decide what you can do to handle your time wasters by employing various techniques to manage your time more effectively. One way in which you will manage your time better is to be assertive. Now you can differentiate between submissive, aggressive and assertive behaviour, this will help you to claim your assertive rights and so behave assertively. Both time management and assertiveness skills will help you to avoid stress; we have also looked at the causes of stress and some techniques for coping with stress.

Review and discussion questions

1 What are the essential requirements for good time management?
2 List five time wasters.

3 Why is an important aspect of time management to research the use of your present time?

4 What is the difference between important and urgent tasks?

5 What is meant by the four 'D's approach?

6 Give four examples of planning tools.

7 Define submissiveness.

8 Define aggressiveness.

9 Define assertiveness.

10 List your assertive rights.

11 What are the advantages of assertive behaviour?

12 'Being assertive can help you to manage your time'. Discuss this statement as applied to the work of a team leader.

13 Describe the time-management practices of someone you know who manages time well. What lessons can be learnt from this person?

14 Discuss the statement that 'the assertive team leader is more effective than the aggressive team leader'. How do people respond to each type of team leader?

15 Aggressive, passive, assertive: what is the difference? How will behaviour of each type, on the part of a team leader, affect the relationship between the team leader and their team?

Case study

Cynthia is not having a good time at the moment; over the last month everything has seemed to go wrong. She has failed her driving test for the third time, she has split up with her boyfriend and her cat was killed in a road accident. You have noticed that Cynthia, who is a member of your workteam has become very irritable, she has told you that she is not sleeping well, she has also started making careless mistakes at work. You have decided to have a word with Cynthia, how will you suggest that she helps herself?

Work-based assignment

Draw up a self-improvement plan indicating how you will manage time, and stress and act in a more assertive way in the future. Review your plan weekly over the next three months.

MANAGING YOURSELF

9 Managing individuals

Learning objectives

On completion of this chapter you will be able to:

- appreciate the complexity of individual behaviour and personality
- explain personality dimensions
- understand the term 'transactional analysis'
- explain the Parent, Adult and Child ego states
- analyse and classify 'transactions'
- recognize the need for adult transactions in the workplace
- appreciate the importance of self-knowledge as a first step to understanding others
- describe and draw a basic model of motivation
- understand and explain Maslow's and Herzberg's motivational models
- understand and explain McGregor's Theory X and Theory Y
- explain the Expectancy Theory
- recognize the signs of a motivated and demotivated team
- describe practical steps that can be taken to motivate your team
- discuss the relationship between pay and motivation.

Introduction

When we first meet other people we can very quickly form an impression of them. We are continually, unconsciously, assessing the personality of people. We are all 'informal' personality theorists. We notice characteristics of their behaviour, their appearance, dress and the way they talk; we then make assumptions about their personalities based on that limited information. This is called 'stereotyping'. Our first impressions of people are very powerful. When we make these judgements we are using our attitudes arising from our experiences and our family and all the people who have influenced us in our life so far. Some examples of stereotyping are:

- fat people are jolly
- Scots are mean
- Americans are loud
- women cry a lot.

Research shows that we are, in fact, very poor judges of personality as stereotypes are usually wrong.

Individual behaviour is complex. You need to have some understanding of aspects of human behaviour to help you understand your staff and yourself better. We are all unique individuals who deal with the world in our own unique ways. But what makes us different from one another? How can we identify and describe the differences and compare individuals with each other? Psychologists have tried to answer these questions using the concept of personality. Personality is a comprehensive, all-embracing concept. The way in which you understand the world and your place in it, the things that motivate you, and the way in which you learn are all aspects of your personality. There has been a great deal of research done on human behaviour and personality.

Another important area that you need to appreciate regarding an individual's behaviour is what motivates individuals at work. This chapter looks at individuals in relation to personality, how individuals interact with one another, and what motivates different people.

Personality

Eysenck is one of the most famous personality theorists. His work was based on the use of questionnaires, from which he measured the respondents' traits and grouped them to produce some overall categories of personality type. This analysis enables comparisons to be made between people.

Eysenck has identified two major dimensions on which personality can vary.

Extrovert or introvert

Extroverts	Introverts
Tough-minded	Tender-minded
Need strong and varied stimulation	Do not need much external stimuli
Act impulsively	Distrust impulse
Optimistic	Pessimistic
Display their emotions	Suppress emotions
Have many friends	Prefer books to people
Unreliable	Reliable
Crave excitement	Have little excitement
Sociable – like parties	Introspective
Carefree	Lead careful, sober lives
Take risks	Plan ahead
Need people to talk to	Withdrawn
Prefer change	Appreciate order
Active	Quiet
Expressive	Reserved
Enjoy practical jokes	Experience strong emotions
Aggressive	Retiring
Quick tempered	Worry about moral standards

Eysenck said that seven personality traits form a cluster which generates the personality type extrovert or introvert. They are:

Extroverts	Introverts
1 Expressiveness	1 Carefulness
2 Impulsiveness	2 Responsibility
3 Risk-taking	3 Control
4 Sociability	4 Reflectiveness
5 Practicality	5 Unsociability
6 Irresponsibility	6 Inhibition
7 Activity	7 Inactivity

Neurotic or stable

Neurotics: emotionally unstable anxious	Stable: emotionally stable adjusted
Low opinion of themselves	Self-confident
Pessimistic	Optimistic
Disappointed with life	Resist irrational fears
Depressed	Easy-going
Upset when things go wrong	Realistic
Worry about things, not self-reliant	Solve their own problems
Imagine they are ill, demand sympathy	Have few health worries
Feel they are failures	Have few regrets about their past
Obsessive, conscientious, finicky	
Highly disciplined, staid	
Dislike untidiness and disorder	

Eysenck said that seven personality traits form a cluster which generates the personality types neurotic or stable. They are:

Neurotic	Stable
1 Low self-esteem	1 Self-esteem
2 Anxiety	2 Calm
3 Guilt	3 Guilt freedom
4 Obsessiveness	4 Casualness
5 Hypochondriasis	5 Sense of health
6 Unhappiness	6 Happiness
7 Lack of autonomy	7 Autonomy

ASSESSING AND DEVELOPING YOUR OWN PERFORMANCE

Eysenck uses a questionnaire with 96 questions, to measure the E and N dimensions. The dimensions are not related to one another, so you can be, for example, a stable extrovert or a stable introvert. Most people do not fall into one category or another of each dimension. We tend to fall somewhere between the two extremes.

Eysenck's work formed the basis of much work that has been done since on psychometric testing, which is a technique being used increasingly in the job selection process or for putting together a balanced team of people whose personalities will complement one another. These tests are very useful for the individual to gain self-knowledge, and can increase understanding of yourself; the test results highlight your strengths and areas for development. Self-knowledge leads to a better understanding of those who work around you.

Transactional analysis

Transactional analysis, or TA as it is known, was originally developed by Eric Berne. It is another way of understanding behaviour. It is based on the belief that we can learn from studying the way in which our decisions and communications are based on our thoughts and feelings. It is based on the idea that each personality, that is all of us, have three ego types:

- Parent
- Adult
- Child.

Each ego state has its own set of feelings, beliefs and behaviour patterns. These states are observable in ourselves and others.

Ego state	Characteristics	How you feel
Parent	Nurturing Controlling Sets rules Limits Rewards Punishes	You feel and behave in ways learnt from mother, father, teachers, you establish rules of conduct and enforce them.
Adult	Rational Thoughtful Controlled Systematic	You observe and collect data, think, weigh probable outcomes of alternative courses of action and make decisions.
Child	Feeling Intuitive Adaptive Energetic Spontaneous	You feel and behave as you did when a child. You experience strong feelings and emotions such as, love, joy, and hate. You are creative, you have fun, adapt to or feel bad about the demands of more powerful people.

Parent ego

The Parent ego works automatically, particularly if you are involved in any critical or evaluation process. The Parent ego has two facets:

The controlling parent	The caring parent
The controlling, disciplining, restricting Parent. Uses phrases like:	The helpful, caring, loving Parent. Uses phrases like:
What will people say? That's the limit Why haven't you? You must never	Don't be afraid I'll help you Oh dear! What a shame Take care

Child ego

The Child ego reacts emotionally with the feelings and instincts of childhood. The Child ego has three facets:

The natural child	The little professor	The adapted child
Primitive, impulsive, instinctive, undisciplined and demanding.	Creative, intuitive and manipulative.	Guilt, rebellion, obedience and compromise.

When in Child ego state, we use phrases like:

I like	I won't
I must	You always try to
Let's play	Help me
It's mine	If she can, so can I.

Adult ego

The Adult ego is the mature and deliberating part of personality. You are sensible and your actions and words are well considered. The Adult ego collects information, evaluates it, tackles and solves problems, all in a calm, logical way. You concentrate on facts, not feelings and prejudices. There is just one facet to the Adult ego. The Adult ego asks questions, seeks out facts by using phrases such as:

What is that?	What do you think?
Why did it happen?	What are the choices?
Let's find out	Let's experiment
Let's define it	How can we handle it best?

Transactions at work

In transactional analysis any form of communication is called a transaction. This analysis is useful, because if you know and understand what the ego states are, you can *choose* the ego state most suitable for the situation. Knowledge of TA can be useful to you if you are dealing with difficult situations. In the majority of work situations, the Adult–Adult transactions are likely to be the norm. You should always aim to transact in an Adult–Adult way. If you respond by adopting the Adult ego state, your work transactions are more likely to involve a rational problem-solving approach and reduce the possibility of conflict.

Activity 46

Classify the following statements as adult, parent or child:

1 You really ought to be more tidy.
2 Don't look at me, I haven't touched it.
3 That's all we need. They'll fire us tomorrow!
4 Let's not spread gossip, we haven't heard it officially yet.
5 Thank you for reminding me. I'll follow it up straight away.
6 Every time we are busy it breaks down. If you knew the problems that we have with this stupid machine!

See Feedback section for answer to this activity.

ASSESSING AND DEVELOPING YOUR OWN PERFORMANCE

Motivation

Much has been written about motivation over the years and a considerable amount of research has been carried out on motivation. This unit considers why people work. An initial reaction if you ask anybody the question, 'Why do you work?', is to answer 'For the money'. But research has indicated that it is not quite as simple as that.

Activity 47

What things in your working life have made you feel really satisfied?

What has made you feel dissatisfied or unhappy?

See Feedback section for answer to this activity.

Motivation is about satisfying the needs that exist within us. Motivation is the drive which causes people to achieve goals which will satisfy their needs. See Figure 9.1 for a basic model of motivation.

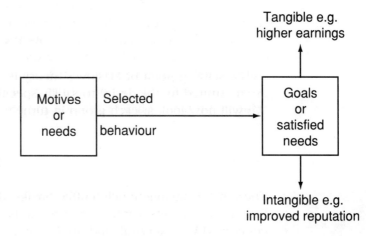

Figure 9.1
A basic model of motivation. Reprinted by permission of Bankers Books. From *Supervisory Skills* by Sally Palmer (1996)

There are many theories of motivation, we will now look at a selection of these.

Maslow's hierarchy of needs

Maslow developed his hierarchy of needs in 1954. He saw human needs at various levels. See Figure 9.2.

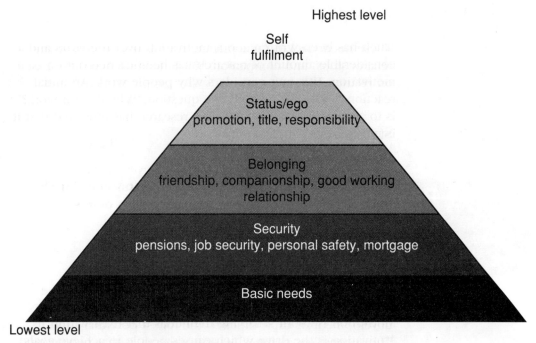

Highest level

Self fulfilment

Status/ego
promotion, title, responsibility

Belonging
friendship, companionship, good working relationship

Security
pensions, job security, personal safety, mortgage

Basic needs

Lowest level

Figure 9.2 Maslow's hierarchy of needs

The starting point of Maslow's theory is that most people are motivated by the desire to satisfy specific groups of needs. We will now look at each group in turn.

Basic

These needs include lunch, coffee breaks, the location of facilities e.g. toilets, canteen, rest room. Basic needs are concerned with survival, and until they have been satisfied they will override any higher needs.

Security

These needs include security procedures, the fire drill, personal and emotional safety, insurance and pension schemes. Security needs are about establishing a stable environment, relatively free from threats.

ASSESSING AND DEVELOPING YOUR OWN PERFORMANCE

Belonging

These needs include acceptance, friendship, good working relationships, and companionship. Belonging needs are based on relationships with others.

Status/ego

These needs include responsibility, achievement, title, confidence, reputation and promotion. Status needs are based on capability and the respect generated from others.

Self-fulfilment

These needs include job satisfaction, and the desire to be creative. Self-fulfilment needs are concerned with the development of capabilities to the fullest potential.
The second key point of Maslow's theory is that people tend to satisfy their needs step-by-step, starting with the basic needs and then moving up the hierarchy. If anything threatens our lower needs, we concentrate on correcting these before moving upwards again.

Herzberg's motivation hygiene theory

Herzberg's work concentrated on job satisfaction. Herzberg said that there were two factors in work motivation:

1 satisfiers – motivating factors
2 dissatisfiers – hygiene factors.

Satisfiers – motivating factors

These factors will motivate people to do their job well:

- achievement
- recognition
- work itself
- responsibility
- advancement.

Dissatisfiers – hygiene factors

These factors will make you feel dissatisfied if there is anything wrong with them, but if they are okay they will not motivate you to do a better job:

- company policy and administration
- supervision
- salary
- interpersonal relations
- working conditions.

See Figure 9.3 for Herzberg's theory.

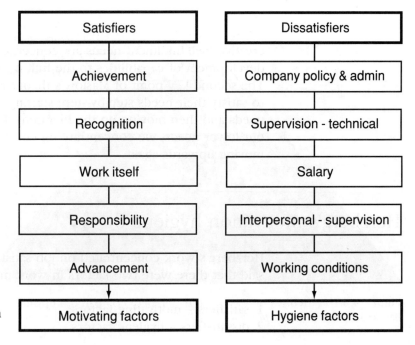

Figure 9.3
Herzberg's motivation
hygiene theory

The work of Maslow and Herzberg compared

The factors which Herzberg used correspond with Maslow's hierarchy of needs. See Figure 9.4 for a diagrammatic representation of both theories.

As a leader, you only have a certain amount of influence over the bottom three levels of Maslow's hierarchy. The three lower levels on Maslow's triangle must usually be satisfied before you can start to motivate individuals.

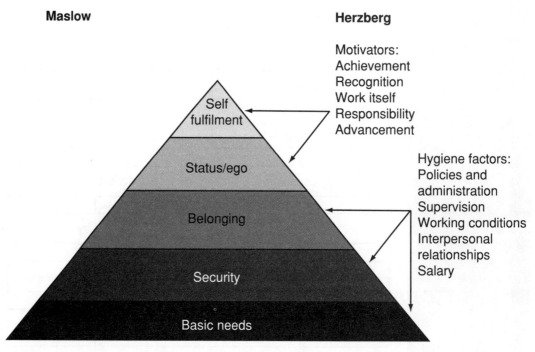

Figure 9.4 The theories of Maslow and Herzberg compared. Reprinted by permission of Bankers Books. From *Supervisory Skills* by Sally Palmer (1996)

PEOPLE AND SELF MANAGEMENT

| Activity 48 | Consider your own motives for wanting to be a team leader. Rank the statements in the left-hand column from 1 to 10 and, with reference to the work of Maslow, categorize each 'motive' statement by its relevant type of need. |

Number	Statement	Your ranking	Need category i.e. basic security, belonging, status/ego or self-fulfilment
1	More money		
2	More influence at work		
3	Greater security of employment		
4	Greater professional status		
5	Greater personal proficiency		
6	Greater career experience		
7	More freedom of action		
8	More responsibility		
9	More recognition		
10	Greater scope of achievement		

Your rankings will indicate what factors motivate you. See Feedback section for answer to this activity.

McGregor's Theory X and Theory Y

In Chapter 5 we looked at the work of Douglas McGregor on motivation and leadership. He suggested that managers behaved in different ways towards their staff and the way in which managers behaved was dependent upon the assumptions they made about the people who worked for them. He suggested that there were two sets of assumptions.

ASSESSING AND DEVELOPING YOUR OWN PERFORMANCE

He called the two sets of assumptions Theory X and Theory Y. Theory X is based on the following assumptions:

- the average person has an inherent dislike of work and will avoid it if possible
- most people prefer to be told what to do
- most people try to avoid responsibility
- most people are not ambitious
- most people just want security and nothing else
- because of this, most people have to be controlled in some way
- control can be achieved by the appropriate use of rewards and punishment.

Theory Y is based on the following assumptions:

- people are capable of exercising self-control and discretion
- the average person is willing to seek and accept responsibility
- people are good at using such qualities as imagination, ingenuity and creativity to the advantage of the organization for which they work
- there are intrinsic rewards (rewards which are derived from self-fulfilment of the individual's personal needs) as well as extrinsic rewards (rewards provided by the organization, such as pay, promotion, good working conditions) related to work and people are attracted to both.

Theory X and Theory Y can be related to Maslow's hierarchy of needs. Theory X, in which people are treated more like objects, relates only to the lower part of the hierarchy. It assumes that satisfying basic and security needs is all that is required. Theory Y, on the other hand, takes the higher levels into account by emphasizing people's maturity, creativity and the need for belonging, status and self-fulfilment.

The Theory X manager will try to motivate staff by:

- using authority
- close supervision
- rules and regulations
- threats and punishments.

It could be said that the Theory X manager is trying to motivate using a *stick*. An alternative and more effective approach to motivation used by managers who use the Theory

Y approach is by using the *carrot*, this is done by using bonus and incentive schemes where good work results in more money and/or benefits. The Theory Y manager will also always treat people fairly.

The expectancy theory

The expectancy theory examines the *process* of motivation and is a result of work done in the USA by V. H. Vroom, E. E. Lawler and L. W. Porter. The theory is based on how a person perceives the relationship between three things: effort, performance and reward.

Motivation $\rightarrow$ Effort $\rightarrow$ Performance $\rightarrow$ Reward

People are *motivated* to put in the *effort* to work by:

the belief that effort at work will lead to effective *performance* the belief that effective performance will lead to *rewards*.

The expectancy theory states that the strength of an individual's motivation to do something will depend on the extent to which the person *expects* (hence the name, expectancy theory) the results of their efforts to contribute towards their personal needs or goals. According to this theory people will decide how much they are going to put into their work according to the value that they place on the expected outcome. For example, a newly appointed member of staff would probably value promotion but would not expect that they have much chance of being promoted so soon. High value, but low expectation. If this person believes that their efforts will not lead to promotion, effort to try to secure promotion is not worthwhile.

Effort or motivated behaviour occurs when a person thinks that the effort will lead to effective performance, which in turn will lead to rewards which are seen as attractive.

However effort does not always result in effective performance. There are various reasons for this, for example, where the individual requires more training or where there are insufficient resources available to perform the task properly.

Effective performance may not always lead to the rewards anticipated by the individual. In large traditional organizations there is often no system for rewarding people individually. Many staff do a very good job but have to wait years to be promoted.

Signs of motivation

The attitude and behaviour of your staff will reflect motivation or lack of it! Motivation can be seen in:

- energy, enthusiasm, determination
- cooperation in achieving results
- willingness to accept responsibility
- acceptance of change
- high results achieved.

Activity 49

List five possible signs of demotivation.

See Feedback section for answer to this activity.

Investigate 15

Well-motivated staff are important to the working of any organization. Does the management of your organization take steps to see that the staff are well motivated? What are those steps? What extra steps could they take?

Practical steps to deal with demotivation

As a team leader, you need to be aware of how you can get your team to work willingly and how to maximize the individual's satisfaction at work. Some practical steps are detailed below.

Make every team member feel valued

- Monitor their work
- share an interest in their lives and whatever they hold important
- create an atmosphere of approval and cooperation
- ensure that every person understands the importance of their contribution to the team and the team's objectives

- ensure that everybody understands the function of the organization, and why the organization is important.

Provide scope for development

- Agree targets for all subordinates
- provide on- and off-the-job training
- arrange any necessary internal and external contacts
- use team members to train other team members in the specialist skills they have
- organize work to use team skills to the fullest
- delegate.

Recognize achievements

- Praise individual success
- report regularly on the team's progress
- regular meetings to monitor and counsel on an individual's progress towards targets
- explain the organization's results and achievements.

Job rotation, job enlargement, job enrichment

Job rotation

It is possible to provide your team with more variety in their work by using a system of job rotation. This is simply switching the team around between a number of jobs so that the team members do not get bored with doing the same job all the time. It is good practice to use job rotation as it means that your team will become multi-skilled and, when people are off sick or on holiday, other members of the team can do their job.

Job enlargement

Job enlargement is about adding more tasks of a similar complexity to an existing job, thereby extending the job. As with job rotation this can make the job less mundane and more interesting.

ASSESSING AND DEVELOPING YOUR OWN PERFORMANCE

Job enrichment

The best way to motivate your team is to enrich their jobs. Job enrichment is a method of motivating your team by adding complexity and variety to the job that they do. Team members can then use more initiative and skills when they are at work, which makes the job more demanding, interesting and motivating for them. Job enrichment offers the opportunity for team members to extend their skills and develop themselves.

Activity 50

Review the work of your section and ask yourself the following questions:

- what work in my area is uninteresting routine?
- what aspects are there which are unusual and/or carry specific responsibility?
- are most of the uninteresting jobs done by the same people?
- does my job include interesting work which others could do?
- do all my staff understand why the work that appears to be mundane is essential to the satisfactory running of the section?
- how often do I show my appreciation for work well done?
- how much of the section's work offers a challenge to the person doing it?
- what can I do to see that as much challenge as possible is built in to the various jobs in my section?
- can I allow the staff to make more decisions in their jobs?
- am I as fully aware as possible of the skills and abilities of the team?
- what is the morale of the staff like? If it is low do I know why? What am I going to do about it?

Use your answers to the above questions to think about what you can do to improve the motivation of your team.

Investigate 16

How does your organization motivate its staff? Are the methods used by your organization effective?

PEOPLE AND SELF MANAGEMENT

Reward and motivation

We all need income to live and the size of our income will affect our standard of living. It is probably true to say that we would all like to earn more money. We are also usually concerned that our pay is fair in comparison with others both inside and outside the organization.

Although one of the main reasons that people go to work is for the money and the whole reward package provided by their employer, there are limitations to money as a form of motivation. See Figure 9.5 for examples of the elements of a reward package. Rates of pay are probably more useful as a means of keeping the organization adequately staffed, rather than as a means of getting them to work harder. Pay is more likely to be a hygiene factor than a motivator. Incentive schemes, such as performance-related pay, bonus payments and profit sharing, are more likely to motivate staff to work harder.

Salary
Pension
Cheap products and services
Holiday
Share option scheme
Relocation allowance
Car
Bonus payments
Profit sharing
Commission

Figure 9.5
Some elements of a
reward package

| Investigate 17 | What does the reward package in your organization consist of? |

Summary

If you know about your own personality and the personalities of the people you work with it can help you to:

- understand your own feelings and behaviour
- gain an impression of how you appear to other people
- understand why people behave in certain ways
- adjust your behaviour to get an appropriate outcome.

Understanding what motivates you and the members of your team can help you to appreciate when your team are feeling motivated and demotivated; if you know this you can take appropriate action to try to ensure that the team you lead is motivated. There is a direct link between motivation and performance, a highly motivated team is a high-performing team. One of the great challenges for you as a team leader is to keep your team motivated; this chapter will have given you an indication of how to recognize the motivation levels of your team and provide some suggestions regarding actions that you can take to ensure that your team is motivated.

Review and discussion questions

1 What is meant by the term 'stereotyping'?
2 Briefly explain the terms 'introvert' and 'extrovert' according to Eysenck.
3 According to Eysenck, what is the 'N' dimension?
4 What is psychometric testing used for?
5 According to Berne, what is a 'transaction'?
6 What are the characteristics of the three ego states, Parent, Adult and Child?
7 What are the two aspects to the parent ego?
8 What are the three aspects to the child ego?
9 Why should workplace transactions be Adult to Adult?
10 How can a knowledge of interpersonal behaviour help you to be a better team leader?
11 Draw a basic model of motivation.

12 List the five levels in Maslow's hierarchy.

13 Briefly compare Maslow's and Herzberg's theories of motivation.

14 Briefly describe McGregor's Theory X and Theory Y managers.

15 It has been said that, ideally, motivation should lead to effort, performance and reward, and so back to motivation. Comment on whether this model really works, relating it to what an organization can do to ensure that it does.

16 'All you need is well-motivated staff'. How do you go about ensuring that your staff are well motivated?

17 'This is a really nice job and the people are great, but there's not enough to do and little chance of promotion.' What motivational theories does this statement suggest to you, and why?

18 List the types of behaviour that demonstrate that a team is motivated.

19 What practical steps can a team leader take to deal with demotivation?

20 'As long as staff get paid at the end of the month, what more do they need in the way of motivation?' Do you believe this statement to be true?

Case study 1	As team leader, you have observed that Brenda, a member of your staff, is having difficulty handling a series of conflict situations with one particular colleague. She tells you that Mr Jones behaves like her father, is always critical and treats her like a child, which makes her feel frustrated and guilty. Explain this situation to Brenda, and suggest some ways in which she can alter the relationship for the better.

Case study 2

Six months ago Sarah Williams retired as team leader in a busy office. Everyone liked her, but she was a 'soft touch', and the office work had become careless, slow and untidy. From the start, her successor, Joanna Brennan, decided to tighten up procedures, mainly by deliberately briefing every staff member, young and old, on every detail of their work, watching every move, accepting no explanations or excuses and reporting staff to management when they were not up to scratch.

Her manager has just congratulated her on getting the work in order, but he has also commented on a noticeable drop in morale: one person has left the team, three have asked for transfers to other teams and the atmosphere is perceptibly cool. 'Well', said Joanna, 'in an odd way it's really good motivation: people like to know where they stand; they appreciate firmness, and I am supposed to be first-line management. Anyway, discipline always achieves results'.

'I think we'd better discuss this question of motivation', said the manager. If you were the manager in question, what would you say to Joanna?

Work-based assignment

C12.1
C12.3

Select job roles that members of your team have. Consider in what ways you can enrich the jobs. Talk to members of your team who carry out the jobs now and incorporate their ideas into re-designed jobs that will provide more interest and opportunities for personal growth for the job holders. Produce a brief report describing the 'old' job, describing how you changed the job and noting any benefits that have been gained by the job holders and the organization following this job enrichment project.

10 Decision making and problem solving

Learning objectives

On completion of this chapter you will be able to:

- describe the importance of making decisions
- list the three levels of decision-making in an organization
- acknowledge that there are different ways of making decisions
- apply the key steps in the decision-making process to a real decision
- understand when it is appropriate to make group decisions
- understand the advantages and disadvantages of group decision making
- list the six stages of the problem-solving model
- use the problem-solving model to solve problems.

Introduction

As a team leader you must be prepared to make decisions. Decision making involves making a choice between alternative courses of action. Your job role will require you to weigh up the alternatives available and decide on the most appropriate. You take many decisions every day spontaneously; these are the repetitive decisions which are part of your present job. Other decisions need more deliberate thought. Sometimes, when you are faced with a decision, your thoughts can be disorganized and, as with problem solving, it can help to have a model to follow to assist you. This is particularly the case if the decision is an important or difficult one.

Although it is very appropriate that some decisions are better made quickly, even instinctively, it often helps to have a logical step-by-step approach to ensure that nothing is overlooked. It also helps to write down the steps. Although it might seem cumbersome, it will help you to assimilate all the facts and select the appropriate action.

Just as we make decisions every day, so we all solve many problems every day of our lives. They are problems which we are used to dealing with on a regular basis. Routine and procedural problems are often solved by learnt methods. Some problems are solved by a process that is so rapid because they are so familiar to us that we solve them almost instantaneously. In this chapter we will look at both decision making and problem solving in more detail.

Types of decisions

There are various levels of decision making within an organization:

- *strategic level* – made by senior managers; for example, deciding the objectives of the organization
- *operational level* – made by managers and supervisors; for example, how to allocate tasks and resources to achieve the objectives of a department
- *individual level* – made by all of us; for example, how we individually can achieve our objectives.

Who should make the decision?

It is also important to consider who should be responsible for making a decision. There is a range of methods that can be used (see Figure 10.1), but no one method is the right method every time. The appropriate method depends on the type of decision that has to be made. It is important to

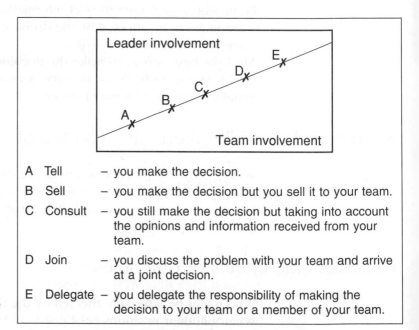

A	Tell	– you make the decision.
B	Sell	– you make the decision but you sell it to your team.
C	Consult	– you still make the decision but taking into account the opinions and information received from your team.
D	Join	– you discuss the problem with your team and arrive at a joint decision.
E	Delegate	– you delegate the responsibility of making the decision to your team or a member of your team.

Figure 10.1
Who should make the decision

consider how quickly the decision needs to be made, how difficult the decision is and the acceptance of the decision by your workteam.

Key steps in decision making

You can use the key steps outlined below to help you make a decision.

Recognize the need for a decision

What is the issue that you need to make a decision about?
Clearly define the issue.
Make sure you are concentrating on the real decision and that you are not getting side-tracked by other issues.

Set criteria for a good decision

What are you trying to achieve?
List how you would gauge a successful outcome.

Gather and analyse the facts and opinions

What facts and information to I need?
From where shall I get it? (Get information from those who are likely to be affected by the decision and from those who are knowledgeable.)
Am I the best person to make the decision?
Do I have the authority to take the decision?
Should I consult with my manager?

Set out and consider alternative courses of action

What alternative possible solutions are there?
What are the advantages and difficulties of each?
List the courses of action and their possible outcomes to assist with comparison.

Consider side effects of outcomes

Who might be adversely affected by the decision?
What will their reactions be?

Make the decision, by reference to criteria, act

Communicate, implement and review

How will I tell everyone concerned so that I get their
   understanding and enthusiasm?
How will I monitor progress?
How will I review the effects of the decision?
Will any modifications be necessary?

Activity 51

Select a work-related decision that you need to make and
analyse the decision using the table below.

Recognize the need for a decision	State the reason you need to make a decision here.
Set criteria for a good decision	Detail the criteria for your decision here.
Gather and analyse the facts and opinions	Note all the relevant facts and opinions.
Set out and consider alternative courses of action	Set out and consider alternative courses of action.
Consider side effects of outcomes	Note the side effects and outcomes of each alternative.
Make the decision, by reference to criteria, act	State your decision.
Communicate, implement and review	Describe how you will communicate, implement and review.

Common faults in decision making

Unfortunately most of us make bad decisions occasionally; it is worth reviewing why this happens. The most common faults in decision making are:

- *delayed decisions* – often due to workload. It is vital to determine which decisions are important and deal with them immediately
- *hurried decisions* – again, often made under pressure. Not enough time is taken to consider all the alternatives
- *indecision* – where people are afraid to commit themselves to a firm decision
- *safe decisions* – not reaching the best decision for the wrong reasons
- *failure to communicate decisions* – a failure to let everybody who needs to know have all the information that they need relating to the decision, when they need it
- *taking a narrow perspective* – the most effective and appropriate options may be missed if the problem solver fails to think broadly, logically and creatively enough.

Group decision making

As already mentioned, managers should not make decisions about every problem. Sometimes it is better to share the decision with a group. Group decisions are made in meetings.

Group decision making should be used when:

- the decision will affect the work of others
- the decision has to be put into effect by others
- information is required from a range of people
- different viewpoints are required
- the person whose responsibility it is cannot think of a satisfactory solution.

Advantages of group decision making

Group decision making enables a wider range of views to be taken into consideration. It will allow more experience, knowledge and attitudes to examine the decision. Discussion within the group may generate new ideas. The adverse consequences of the decision on other individuals or groups are much less likely to be overlooked if a number of people are involved in making the decision.

Disadvantages of group decision making

Making decisions in groups takes longer and so ties up valuable time which is more costly for the organization. There is also a risk of argument and bitterness within the group that is making the decision, particularly if there is a wide range of strongly held views.

Problem solving

Activity 52

Think of three examples of problems that you have encountered today and solved very rapidly because you are familiar with the type of problem.

However, we all have problems to deal with from time to time that are new to us or that are more major and important than the problems we are used to. Examples of the types of problems which might arise in the workplace are: problems concerned with the relationships between the members of your workteam, problems with customers, problems resulting from staff being transferred out of your team or leaving the organization, problems with the technological equipment that you use to make your product or deliver your services.

Some problems can be prevented. We have already looked at the importance of planning; sometimes problems occur when they need not because time was not spent planning in advance. For example, if your office is having a new computer system installed over a weekend it is sensible to make contingency plans just in case the system is not up and running when you return to work on Monday morning. Always try to make sure that problems do not occur in the first place. However well we plan, though, problems do crop up from time to time that we could not have planned for. It is helpful to use a model which suggests a series of steps that you can use to solve problems.

The stages of problem solving

The model shown in Figure 10. 2 suggests six stages that can be used to solve problems..

1 **Recognize** the existence of your problem	Early detection of problems is important: the earlier that you recognize that a problem exists, the less likely it is to grow into a major problem, providing that you act immediately
2 Set **criteria** for a good solution to the problem	Set out criteria for a good solution
3 **Gather information**	Gather relevant facts and opinions
4 **Analyse** the facts and consider **alternative solutions**	Analyse facts in relation to the problem Set out and consider alternative solutions Consider side effects of outcomes Calculate the expected values of solutions
5 **Solve the problem**	Solve the problem, select the best solution by reference to criteria
6 **Communicate, implement and evaluate**	Act, communicate, monitor

Figure 10.2 A six-stage problem-solving model. Reprinted by permission of Bankers Books. From *Supervisory Skills* by Sally Palmer (1996)

Now we will look at each stage in the problem-solving process in more detail.

Recognize the existence of your problem

You always need to be on the look out for problems. The earlier we latch onto a potential problem, the easier we will find it to deal with. Although we need to be on the look out for problems we must not imagine that problems exist when they do not. It is about finding a balance, asking yourself: is this a problem that I need to do something about? Am I overreacting? Is it a genuine problem that needs solving? It often helps to write the problem down so that you can clearly define exactly what the problem is. Once you have established that you definitely do have a problem that requires a solution, you can move onto the next stage of the process.

Set the criteria for a good solution to the problem

You need to decide exactly what the features of a good solution to the problem are. You need to know clearly what the desired outcome is. For example, let us take an imagined problem. Assume that you are looking for a new suite of offices.

Your requirements might be:

- rental cost of maximum £500 per month
- within 5 miles of existing premises
- at least 1000 sq. ft
- at least 150 sq. ft of storage
- at least three offices.

These are the criteria for a good solution to the problem. Finding a satisfactory solution might not be that simple. You might find some premises which fulfil all the criteria except the cost is £750 per month. Another office suite might be in the right price range but have insufficient storage space. In this case, you might have to rank the criteria from the most important to the least important. As you cannot find a solution that meets all the criteria, you may have to select the one that scores the highest once you have weighted the criteria.

Gather information

The next stage is to gather the facts. You need to try and do this with an open mind, ensure that you do not pre-judge the situation, ensure that you have enough information; again it helps to write down all the information you have gleaned.

Analyse the facts and consider alternative solutions

Now it is time to analyse all the information you have gathered. Is there any information you have collected that is biased? Have you got rid of all your prejudices? Is all the information that you have gathered accurate? Have you seen a similar problem before? Could your experience in solving this similar problem help? Are you concentrating too much on the detail of the problem and not looking at the whole picture? Can you draw a diagram of the problem? Do you need to ask someone to look at the problem with you? A fresh approach may help to generate a solution. Question everything, keep asking why? Look at the problem from as many points of view as possible.

Solve the problem

Select the solution that meets the criteria you have set down for a good solution and one that minimizes any undesirable side effects.

Communicate, implement and evaluate

Now that the solution has been selected, you need to act. Do whatever it is that you have decided to do. Ensure that you have clearly communicated your solution to everybody who needs to know. Ensure that you set up a system to review how things are going, to check out that your solution is working and be ready to make adjustments if there is a detail that you have overlooked. Ensure that you have taken steps to make sure that the problem will not recur. Finally, review how you have performed whilst solving the problem. Did you define the problem correctly? Did you manage to gather and analyse the information without bias? Was your solution a good one? What have you learnt?

Figure 10.3 gives an example of how a problem was solved using the problem-solving model.

1 **Recognize** the existence of your problem	You and three of your friends have decided to go on a summer holiday together. You need to decide where you are going to go. This is the problem
2 Set **criteria** for a good solution to the problem	You need to clearly identify what you want out of the holiday, so you meet one night to discuss the criteria. You know that the maximum each of you can spend is £600, plus spending money. The place must be sunny, you require a sandy beach and a hotel which is within walking distance of the beach. You must be able to fly from Manchester Airport and you will not go anywhere where there is any unrest and so the chance of a war. You want to go for two weeks and fly on 14, 15 or 16 July
3 **Gather the information**	You go to three travel agents and tell them what your criteria are. The travel agents provide you with all the information that they have on holidays that might meet your requirements
4 **Analyse** the facts and consider **alternative** solutions	You consider the alternative solutions and the side effects of outcomes. Some places take much longer to fly to and some flights are in the early hours of the morning. Some holidays are cheaper than others
5 **Solve the problem**	You keep the criteria that you set down at the beginning of the process and solve your problem by selecting the most appropriate solution by reference to criteria
6 **Communicate, implement and evaluate**	You book the holiday which fulfils the criteria, you all book your time off at work, you pay your deposit. One of you coordinates all the activities, communicates with all the others to make sure that you all know what is happening. You reflect after your holiday whether the criteria were right for you as a group and use the experience that you have gained this year when you plan your holiday for next year

Figure 10.3 Solving a problem - an example. Reprinted by permission of Bankers Books. From *Supervisory Skills* by Sally Palmer (1996)

PEOPLE AND SELF MANAGEMENT

Summary

In this chapter we have looked at two models, one for decision making and one for problem solving. On most occasions you will make decisions and solve problems quickly, relying on your past experience, but sometimes a decision is more difficult to make or a problem more difficult to solve. This chapter has provided you with guidance you can use to tackle the more difficult issues you encounter at work.

Review and discussion questions

1 In what circumstances is it useful to use a decision-making model?
2 List the three decision-making levels in organizations.
3 What are the five levels of leader involvement in decision making?
4 Why is it not appropriate to always use one level of involvement in decision making?
5 List the key steps in the decision-making process.
6 What factors do you need to consider when gathering and analysing facts and opinions related to the decision?
7 How do you select the criteria for a good decision?
8 Why is it important to tell everyone concerned the outcome of the decision?
9 What are the common faults in decision making?
10 When should group decision making be used?
11 What are the advantages of group decision making?
12 'People spend too much time thinking about decisions; surely the essence of good decisions is to make them firmly and quickly, and get on with the work.' Comment on this statement.
13 Discuss an ideal method for making group decisions. Are any decisions are made on a group basis where you work, what type of decisions are they? Compare the way they are made with your ideal method, and say how the existing method can be improved.
14 'To be decisive means being able to make decisions instinctively.' Comment on the validity of this statement.
15 List the six stages of the problem-solving model.
16 Why does it help to write a problem down?
17 What questions do you need to ask yourself when analysing the facts surrounding a problem?
18 Why is it important to evaluate the problem-solving process?
19 Discuss the suggestion that problem solving is a skill you can learn.

20 If someone suggested to you that you do not need to think too much about solving problems, just make sure that you are good at trouble-shooting, how would you reply?

Case study

Your organization has just designated a large room at the factory where you work as a staff social area. With some investment it could have many uses; £10 000 has been allocated to be spent on the refurbishment.

You are a member of a committee assembled to decide what to do with the room. What steps would you suggest the committee takes to make a good decision? Illustrate each step by reference to the refurbishment of the room.

Work-based assignment

Use the model that has been introduced to you in this chapter to reflect on a work-related problem that you need to solve. Try to solve the problem by completing the boxes below.

1 **Recognize the existence of your problem**	Clearly state the problem
2 **Set criteria for a good solution to the problem**	Set out criteria for a good solution
3 **Gather information**	Gather relevant facts and opinions
4 **Analyse the facts and consider alternative solutions**	Analyse facts in relation to the problem, set out and consider alternative solutions, consider side effects of outcomes
5 **Solve the problem**	Select your solution
6 **Communicate, implement and evaluate**	Plan how you would act, communicate and monitor the situation

11 Working with others

Learning objectives

On completion of this chapter you will be able to:

- understand the need for constructive working relationships
- appreciate the growth of recognition of the importance of counselling in business organizations
- differentiate between counselling and advice
- recognize situations when counselling will be beneficial
- explain how to prepare for, and conduct, a counselling interview
- understand the skills required to conduct a counselling interview
- explain why rules at work are necessary
- outline a typical disciplinary procedure process
- describe some common reasons for invoking the disciplinary procedure
- explain how to conduct a disciplinary interview
- outline a typical grievance procedure process
- appreciate what is meant by the term 'employee relations'
- understand the role of trade unions
- describe various methods of employee participation
- appreciate the causes, advantages and disadvantages of conflict.

Introduction

In this chapter we will examine the importance of developing a constructive working relationship between you and your team, you and your other colleagues and between members of your workteam. Sometimes, unfortunately, things do go wrong and you need to know how to handle these difficult situations when they arise.

Constructive working relationships

As the team leader you have an important impact on the quality of personal relationships in your team. If there are good relationships between you and the rest of your team, and good relationships within your team, it will be much easier for you to perform effectively as a team and achieve both your personal and your team goals.

You need to develop a rapport with your team; this rapport helps you to understand each other and communicate effectively with each other. You will develop a rapport firstly, by knowing and understanding yourself (the work that you did in Chapter 7 will have helped you with this). The second way in which you will develop rapport is by employing many of the interpersonal skills we have looked at already: communication skills, the skill of assertiveness and giving constructive and honest feedback to your team. Your team and all your colleagues need to know that you have respect for them, an empathy with them and that you are honest in your dealings with them.

Counselling at work

It was not long ago that counselling was considered to have no place in the workplace. However, counselling at work has now become recognized as an important function of a manager. Organizations have become more concerned with the overall well-being of their staff. Businesses have found that training managers in counselling skills can have very positive benefits, such as reducing absenteeism and gaining employee commitment and motivation. Some large organizations employ their own professional counsellors, others buy in the services of external counselling organizations which can be contacted by telephone – if necessary a face-to-face appointment can be arranged, and the service is often available to staff and their families. The service is entirely confidential.

We are concerned here with the team leader's role in counselling in relation to their workteam, and we will look at how to recognize a counselling need and how to conduct a counselling interview.

Counselling and advice

Counselling is not the same as advice. Advice is where you apprise yourself of the facts and advise somebody what to do in a (usually difficult) situation. Counselling is about encouraging another person to talk about themselves so that they can work out their own solution to their problem.

Counselling involves an interview, but the interview is non-directive, that means that broad general questions are discussed so that the interviewee talks freely and in depth. The counselling interview is usually used to resolve specific problems.

Counselling is a profession in its own right and although this section will give you a framework and advise you of some skills that you can use for counselling in the workplace to help others, there may be a situation when you need to recommend to a person that they seek the services of a professional counsellor.

Recognizing the need for a counselling interview

Sometimes you might know that a member of your team has a problem in their private life which is having an adverse effect on their work. Sometimes the work of somebody in your section is not up to standard or they are constantly late for work or constantly arguing with members of the team. Obviously in these circumstances you need to take some action to rectify the situation; the best place to start is to conduct a counselling interview.

Preparing for the interview

It is important that you choose an appropriate, quiet and private location for a counselling interview and ensure that you are not disturbed. You must also make sure you have allowed enough time for the interview to take place as the speaker must not feel rushed or hurried if you are to get to the bottom of their problem.

Objectives of the counselling interview

It is important for the counsellor to listen very carefully and make every effort to understand the other person's perspective. It is important that the counsellor helps the person they are interviewing to:

- tell their story
- focus on their problem

- look for new perspectives
- clarify the issue
- identify areas for change
- set goals
- develop action plans
- review progress.

The above framework will encourage the speaker to develop their own solutions and enable you to identify areas in which you can support your team member to carry out their action plan. It is important that you remember to review progress and continue to offer support where this is required.

Counselling skills

Counselling requires very specific skills. To achieve the objectives of the counselling interview you need to:

- show empathy with the speaker – empathy is about listening carefully, understanding the important messages and making sure that the person knows that you are understanding their perspective
- not make judgements
- listen carefully to the full story
- try to understand the feelings and emotions behind the person's story
- question with care, using open questions
- reflect back, summarize and re-frame (or paraphrase) – these are ways of checking that you have understood what the other person is saying, they also demonstrate that you are listening and have an empathy with the person. *Reflecting back* is repeating, in similar words, what has been said to you. *Summarizing* is checking and clarifying what the speaker has said by providing a summary to the person, they can then check that you have understood. *Reframing* or *paraphrasing* is saying what the person said but in a different way. It is similar to summarizing but it might start with a phrase such as, 'It sounds almost as if . . .'; phrasing the issue in another way
- use appropriate body language – to indicate that the speaker has your full attention and to encourage them to keep talking.

Rules at work

Clear rules at work benefit both employers and employees. It is important that team leaders are aware of organizational rules and the procedures for dealing with those who break the rules. Rules set standards of conduct at work. It is important to have rules at work to ensure that everybody knows what is expected of them and that things run smoothly. Rules at work usually cover areas such as:

* time keeping
* absence
* health and safety
* misconduct
* use of the organization's facilities
* discrimination
* security.

Rules need to be communicated clearly to all the staff. They need to be written down, readily available – particularly to new employees, rules should also be non-discriminatory and reviewed from time to time to ensure that they are still relevant and to check if any new rules need to be added. Those responsible for applying the rules of the organization, such as team leaders, should be trained appropriately to ensure that they know the rules and deal with staff fairly.

Activity 53

What are the rules at your place of employment? Are they clearly communicated, written down, accessible, non-discriminatory and regularly reviewed?

Organizations need to have systems in place to deal with situations where staff do not adhere to the rules. In the most serious situations the organization's disciplinary procedure may have to be used. There also has to be a system in place to deal with the situation where a member of staff feels that they are being treated unfairly – in these cases the organization's grievance procedure is designed to help.

Disciplinary procedures

A disciplinary procedure helps to ensure that the rules are followed and standards are maintained. It provides a method of dealing with breaches of the rules and can help someone

WORKING WITH OTHERS

who is not performing well to become more effective at work. The disciplinary procedure needs to be applied fairly and consistently within the organization, this will ensure that standards are maintained across the organization.

Paragraph 10 of the ACAS Code of Practice recommends what disciplinary procedures should contain. This is shown in Figure 11.1.

Figure 11.1
What should disciplinary procedures contain? Reproduced with kind permission from The ACAS Code of Practice 1, *Disciplinary Practice and Procedures in Employment*

Disciplinary procedures should:

(a) Be in writing.
(b) Specify to whom they apply.
(c) Provide for matters to be dealt with quickly.
(d) Indicate the disciplinary actions which may be taken.
(e) Specify the levels of management which have the authority to take the various forms of disciplinary action, ensuring that immediate superiors do not normally have the power to dismiss without reference to senior management.
(f) Provide for individuals to be informed of the complaints against them and to be given an opportunity to state their case before decisions are reached
(g) Give individuals the right to be accompanied by a trade union representative or by a fellow employee of their choice
(h) Ensure that, except for gross misconduct, no employees are dismissed for a first breach of discipline.
(i) Ensure that disciplinary action is not taken until the case has been carefully investigated.
(j) Ensure that individuals are given an explanation for any penalty imposed.
(k) Provide a right of appeal and specify the procedure to be followed.

Investigate 18

To what extent do the disciplinary procedures in your organization reflect those recommended by ACAS? How do they differ?

The main aim of disciplinary action is to encourage an employee who is performing unsatisfactorily to improve performance at work. It is important to deal with problems early before they are allowed to develop into more serious problems.

Every organization will write its own disciplinary procedure. An example of a disciplinary procedure is shown in Figure 11.2.

DISCIPLINARY PROCEDURE

(1) Purpose and scope

This procedure is designed to help and encourage all employees to achieve and maintain standards of conduct, attendance and job performance. The company rules (a copy of which is displayed in the office) and this procedure apply to all employees. The aim is to ensure consistent and fair treatment for all.

(2) Principles

a) No disciplinary action will be taken against an employee until the case has been fully investigated.

b) At every stage in the procedure the employee will be advised of the nature of the complaint against him or her and will be given the opportunity to state his or her case before any decision is made.

c) At all stages the employee will have the right to be accompanied by a shop steward, employee representative or work colleague during the disciplinary interview.

d) No employee will be dismissed for a first breach of discipline except in the case of gross misconduct when the penalty will be dismissal without notice or payment in lieu of notice.

e) An employee will have the right to appeal against any disciplinary penalty imposed.

f) The procedure may be implemented at any stage if the employee's alleged misconduct warrants such action.

(3) The Procedure

Minor faults will be dealt with informally but where the matter is more serious the following procedure will be used:

Stage 1 – Oral warning

If conduct or performance does not meet acceptable standards the employee will normally be given a formal ORAL WARNING. He or she will be advised of the reason for the warning, that it is the first stage of the disciplinary procedure and of his or her right of appeal. A brief note of the oral warning will be kept but it will be spent after .... months, subject to satisfactory conduct and performance.

Stage 2 – Written warning

If the offence is a serious one, or if a further offence occurs, a WRITTEN WARNING will be given to the employee by the supervisor. This will give details of the complaint, the improvement required and the timescale. It will warn that action under Stage 3 will be considered if there is no satisfactory improvement and will advise of the right of appeal. A copy of this written warning will be kept by the supervisor but it will be disregarded for disciplinary purposes after .... months subject to satisfactory conduct and performance.

Stage 3 – Final written warning or disciplinary suspension

If there is still a failure to improve and conduct or performance is still unsatisfactory, or if the misconduct is sufficiently serious to warrant only one written warning but insufficiently serious to justify dismissal (in effect both first and final written warning), a FINAL WRITTEN WARNING will normally be given to the employee. This will give details of the complaint, will warn that dismissal will result if there is no satisfactory improvement and will advise of the right of appeal. A copy of this final written warning will be kept by the supervisor but it will be spent after .... months (in exceptional cases the period may be longer) subject to satisfactory conduct and performance.

Alternatively, consideration will be given to imposing a penalty of a disciplinary suspension without pay for up to a maximum of five working days.

Stage 4 – Dismissal

If conduct or performance is still unsatisfactory and the employee still fails to reach the prescribed standards, DISMISSAL will normally result. Only the appropriate Senior Manager can take the decision to dismiss. The employee will be provided, as soon as reasonably practicable, with written reasons for dismissal, the date on which employment will terminate and the right of appeal.

(4) Gross misconduct

The following list provides examples of offences which are normally regarded as gross misconduct:

theft, fraud, deliberate falsification of records
fighting, assault on another person
deliberate damage to company property
serious incapability through alcohol or being under the influence of illegal drugs
serious negligence which causes unacceptable loss, damage or injury
serious act of insubordination
unauthorised entry to computer records.

If you are accused of an act of gross misconduct, you may be suspended from work on full pay, normally for no more than five working days, while the company investigates the alleged offence. If, on completion of the investigation and the full disciplinary procedure, the company is satisfied that gross misconduct has occurred, the result will normally be summary dismissal without notice or payment in lieu of notice.

(5) Appeals

An employee who wishes to appeal against a disciplinary decision should inform .... within two working days. The Senior Manager will hear all appeals and his/her decision is final. At the appeal any disciplinary penalty imposed will be reviewed but it cannot be increased.

Figure 11.2 Disciplinary procedure – an example. Reproduced with kind permission from The ACAS Advisory Handbook *Discipline at Work*, March 1997

Notes on the disciplinary procedure illustrated in Figure 11.2:

1 the procedure will state what constitutes gross misconduct, you will notice that the penalties for gross misconduct are stated in the procedure
2 it is not necessary to work through the procedure in stages, the stage at which the procedure starts will depend on the seriousness of the breach of discipline. For example, a serious breach of discipline may result in a final written warning, when an oral warning or written warning have not been previously given.

The disciplinary procedure is invoked when the employee breaks the rules. Often it is you, the team leader, who is first informed or first notices that a member of your team has broken the rules, for example, by being late for work or breaking health and safety rules. You have to decide what you are going to do about it. You may make a decision that you do not wish to take formal disciplinary action and have a quiet word with your team member. You may decide to warn them about their behaviour and tell them that you will start formal disciplinary proceedings if it happens again. In some circumstances you may make a decision that you need to counsel the employee to establish why the problem arose and help them to recognize what needs to be done to improve their own performance themselves. However, in some circumstances it will be necessary to start formal disciplinary proceedings. The disciplinary procedure will state what constitutes gross misconduct. The usual penalty for gross misconduct is summary dismissal. According to a survey conducted in 1995 by the IRS (Industrial Relations Service) the ten most common disciplinary offences were:

1 absenteeism
2 poor performance
3 poor time-keeping
4 refusal to obey a reasonable instruction
5 theft/fraud
6 sexual/racial harassment
7 verbal abuse
8 health and safety infringements
9 fighting
10 alcohol/drug abuse.

The investigation

It is important that you investigate the incident as soon as possible. You will need to gather all the relevant facts relating to the incident quickly, so that people do not forget what happened. If it looks as though the matter is serious, this will involve taking statements from people and collecting any documentary evidence. If the case you are investigating is one of gross misconduct, you may wish to consider suspension with pay while the investigation is conducted. It is vital to keep very clear, detailed records throughout the investigation and at every step of the disciplinary process – you may have to rely on them in the future.

You are notified of or notice a disciplinary offence	Find out the facts. Make a decision as to whether you need to take any action or not. You may decide, at this stage, that the matter is unimportant and there is no need to take matters further	No action required
	You may decide that the employee would benefit from counselling	Conduct counselling session
	You may decide that the matter is serious and that you need to invoke the disciplinary procedure	Start disciplinary proceedings

The disciplinary interview

If you decide to start disciplinary proceedings, a disciplinary interview will have to be arranged.

Preparing for the interview

Ensure that the individual knows the nature of the complaint and the interview that they will be attending is a disciplinary interview.

Remind the employee that they can bring a representative to the meeting.

Arrange for another team leader, manager or member of the personnel department to attend the meeting.

Make sure that you have all the facts.

Try not to prejudge.

Guard against bias.

Allow adequate time for the interview.

Plan how you will approach the meeting.

Know the disciplinary procedure.

Ensure that you will be undisturbed during the interview and that the venue is suitable.

Check the employee's record.

Conducting the interview

Tell the employee the purpose of the interview.

Let the interviewee know that this is part of the disciplinary procedure.

Make sure the interviewee knows the nature of the complaint and knows about the supporting evidence that you have collected.

Give the interviewee the opportunity to state their case.

Ask open questions.

Probe.

Clarify the organization's situation.

Listen carefully and take notes.

Keep calm and be firm but fair.

If any new facts emerge, decide whether a further investigation is required.

At this stage adjourn the interview.

Consider, with your colleague all of the information that you have collected and decide if you have enough information to make your decision. If you do not, conduct a further investigation and reconvene the meeting at a later date. If you do have enough information, you need to decide what action to take.

Before you decide on the penalty consider the following:

- does the disciplinary procedure give you any guidance?
- what has happened in similar cases in the past?
- what is the employee's disciplinary record like, have there been any similar incidents in the past?
- are there any mitigating circumstances?

Disciplinary penalties:

- In the case of minor offences a *formal oral warning* should be given and the person should be told that this has been noted on the person's record.
- If, over a period of time, the individual has already received one or more oral warnings or the offence is more serious, a *formal written warning* should be given.
- If the employee has received a previous written warning or the offence is considered to be even more serious, a *final written warning* may be given or a disciplinary penalty such as a *disciplinary transfer, disciplinary suspension without pay, demotion, loss of seniority, loss of increment* (providing the contract of employment allows these).
- There may be circumstances where the misconduct warrants only one written warning which is both the first and the final written warning.
- The disciplinary procedure will state how long warnings are valid for. Typically, warnings for minor offences are valid for up to six months and final warnings are valid for 12 months. After the stated periods the warnings cease to be considered when taking into account a future breach of discipline. It is important to be aware of the past disciplinary history of an individual so that if a pattern is emerging of deteriorating performance just after a valid period for a warning expires, you can take this into consideration, perhaps by varying the valid period of a warning.
- If the individual's performance has not improved over a period of time despite warnings the employee can be *dismissed with a period of notice* or payment in lieu of notice.
- If the employee has committed a gross misconduct offence, the employee can be *dismissed without notice*.

Reconvene the interview.

Inform the individual of the decision.
Let the employee know the situation regarding the right of appeal.
If you have given a warning explain exactly what improvement is expected, how long the warning will last and the consequences of failing to improve.

Follow-up

Write up notes immediately.

Unless you have given an oral warning, confirm your decision regarding any action to be taken in writing to the individual, copy to their representative and keep a record.

Monitor future conduct/job performance. Remember the idea of using the disciplinary procedure is to improve job performance.

Make an appointment for a follow-up interview.

Take any action that you agreed.

Let the personnel department know.

Grievance procedures

Collective disputes are usually dealt with by the union, grievance procedures are used for handling individual disputes. The grievance procedure gives the employee the opportunity to raise a grievance and have it dealt with in a structured way. The purpose of an organization having a grievance procedure is to settle a grievance at work at the earliest possible stage. Obviously, most disputes are resolved without invoking the grievance procedure. Ideally the grievance should be dealt with as close to its source as possible. A typical grievance procedure is shown in Figure 11.3.

1 Employee raises grievance with immediate line manager (usually the team leader).
2 If the matter is not settled it is taken to the next level of management. The employee may be accompanied by a friend or trade union representative.
3 If the matter is still not resolved it is taken to senior management, the employee may take a representative.
4 If the employee is still not satisfied, the employee may appeal to the Managing Director.

Figure 11.3
A typical grievance procedure

Each stage of the grievance procedure should have a time limit. This will indicate the time within which the aggrieved employee must have a reply. Written records should be kept at each stage.

Investigate 19

To what extent does the grievance procedure in your organization reflect that shown in Figure 11.3?

The grievance interview

If a member of your team has a grievance, you will probably be the person to conduct the first interview.

Preparing for the interview

Prior to the interview, find out as much as you can about the grievance, what are the facts? How does everybody involved feel about the situation?

If you need to, consult other people for advice.

Check the staff file of the person taking out the grievance, have there been any previous similar situations?

Check the organization's grievance procedure, make sure you follow it.

Make sure that you have a private room and an undisturbed venue for the interview.

Conducting the interview

Aim for a win/win solution.

Be calm but positive.

Allow the interviewee to 'let off steam' first.

Listen carefully to the grievance side of the story.

Summarize from time to time to ensure your mutual understanding of the exact situation and the facts.

Listen carefully, probe deeply.

Attempt to unravel the cause(s) of the grievance.

Do not belittle the issue or dismiss it.

Finish with positive action for the future, make sure that you both know what will happen next.

Consider the actions to be taken and assess their consequences.

Follow-up

Investigate the facts and possible course of action.

Write up the notes of the meeting.

Follow up the interview with appropriate actions.

Let the personnel department know.

WORKING WITH OTHERS

Industrial tribunals

In some cases, disciplinary procedures may result in dismissal. If an employee feels that they have been treated unfairly they can take the matter to an industrial tribunal. Industrial tribunals deal with cases where an employee thinks that they have a case against their employer in respect of the various rights available to them under the employment protection and anti-discrimination laws. If successful, the employee may receive financial compensation or reinstatement, re-engagement or another suitable remedy. Usually prior to a case being heard by the tribunal, ACAS – the Advisory, Conciliation and Arbitration Service – attempts to conciliate between the two parties to try to obtain a mutually acceptable outcome. Only if this is not possible is the case heard by the tribunal.

Employee relations

Trade unions deal with employee relations. The term 'employee relations' refers to the interrelationships between managers and those people they manage, both the formal and informal relationships. The term 'employee relations' has a wider scope than that of 'industrial relations'. Industrial relations is mainly concerned with collective bargaining. Collective bargaining is about employees working together as a group to negotiate with the employer about such matters as rules at work and employment conditions, including pay.

Employee relations is about:

- pay – collective bargaining
- working conditions
- working procedures and rules
- redundancy plans or expansion and recruitment plans
- promotion policy
- fair treatment of members
- employee welfare
- training and development of employees
- social responsibility
- grievance and disciplinary policy
- communications policy
- worker participation – joint decision-making.

The role of the trade unions

Trade unions are organized associations of workers established for the protection of their common interest. A trade union must be recognized by its members' employer as an organization with which the employer is prepared to negotiate.

The role of the trade union is to promote and protect the interests of its members. In carrying out this role they work to:

- formulate and express the collective views of the members
- seek to develop an environment which assures secure employment
- improve physical conditions at work, including monitoring health and safety
- ensure equitable treatment
- protect members' standards of living
- develop machinery for communication and involvement at work
- encourage the most efficient use of all resources
- be involved in the wider social, political and economic activities of the nation.

Union members pay a subscription to their union, which is how the union raises the funds it needs to finance its activities.

Most unions have a head office and are organized into areas or regions, each area or region has a number of branches which might be composed of union members working in one organization or one small geographical area. Trade unions have officers that might be employed at head office and/or at area level; these are full-time paid officials employed by the union to carry out its policies. They often have voluntary officials elected to be branch officers of the union in a particular area and/or representatives in the workplace. The trade union officers working in the workplace are sometimes called shop stewards in manufacturing industries and office representatives in office-based, service organizations.

The team leader and the shop steward or office representative

Team leaders are often in direct contact with the staff and so are at the sharp end of employee relations. Involvement may include discussions about changes in work procedures or newly introduced rules, meeting union representatives as they sit in on disciplinary meetings or grievance meetings. A member of staff will approach the office representative in the first instance if they have a problem and the staff representative will either deal with the matter directly with you or contact the union central office for advice. You should always know who the staff representative is in your workplace, and make sure that they are informed of all pertinent events affecting their members.

Investigate 20   Which unions represent staff who work for your organization? Are all the unions recognized by your organization?

Employee participation

The British Institute of Management (now the Institute of Management) published a report in 1977, entitled 'Employee Participation – the way ahead'. In that report participation was described as:

> . . . *the practice in which employees take part in management decisions and it is based on the assumption that the community of interest between employer and employee is furthering the long term prospects of the enterprise and those working in it.*

Employee involvement has been recognized, over recent years, as being very important. It began to flourish in the 1980s. At this time, the most important mechanisms for employee involvement were quality circles and job enrichment schemes (designed to make work more interesting). Quality circles became quite popular in the UK although they had mixed success. A variety of employee involvement schemes emerged, including financial participation, such as employee share option schemes and profit sharing schemes. Most recently, various forms of teamworking have become popular, based around customer care and total quality management. These schemes focus very much on problem solving.

There is a range of employee participation schemes as shown in Figure 11.4.

Share options/ profit sharing	Consultation	Job enrichment	Empowerment by delegation	Collective bargaining	Works council	Employee directors

Low power/ influence	← ————————————————————————————————→	Greater power/ influence

Figure 11.4 Range of options for employee participation. Reproduced from *Personnel Management*, fourth edition (1997) by G. A. Cole by permission of Letts Educational

Activity 54

How does your organization involve its employees? Complete the following table.

Type of participation	How my organization involves its employees
Share options/ profit sharing	
Consultation	
Job enrichment	
Empowerment by delegation	
Collective bargaining	
Works council	
Employee directors	

Managing conflict

The focus of this chapter, and of the whole book, has been on encouraging positive working relationships with colleagues. However, there are bound to be occasions when your team disagree with one another and with you as the team leader. This type of conflict is not always a bad thing: if you and your team are to have an open and constructive relationship, you must all feel that you can express your ideas freely. Conflict is healthy and constructive. It can lead to good ideas and better ways of working; if you have openness and trust within the team conflict will result.

Activity 55	List the benefits that you think will result from your team feeling that they can express their disagreements openly.

See Feedback section for answer to this activity.

Common causes of conflict

A writer, Herbert S. Kindler, in his book *Managing Disagreement Constructively*, identified four main causes of conflict:

1 *Inaccurate or incomplete information*. People can only base their opinions and feelings on the information that they have. If people do not have complete and accurate information they may be interpreting a situation in different ways, which can lead to conflict. This is why it is so important to have open communication between you and your team and within your team. How many times can you recall that conflict has occurred because somebody has got the wrong message and so the wrong idea about something.

2 *Inappropriate or seemingly incompatible goals*. It is important that your goals, the goals of the team and the goals of each team member in the organization, are compatible. It is important that you all have shared values and a shared purpose if the team is to minimize conflict.

3 *Ineffective or unacceptable methods*. Kindler suggests that if the team's objectives and success criteria are confused, or if team members are given inadequate support, the result is disarray. Some members do not act according to principles established by the group. This is unacceptable to other members of the group and so can lead to conflict.

4 *Antagonistic or other negative feelings*. If there are long standing resentments and hostilities within the team a small incident can re-ignite negative feelings. That is why it is important to resolve conflicts as soon as they occur so that negative feelings do not fester.

Resolving conflicts

Kindler suggests four principles to be maintained in the resolution of conflicts:

1 *Maintain respect for others and yourself*. Do not show a lack of respect for others, always stick to the issues, never resort to personal abuse.
2 *Empathize with the other person*. Try to understand how the other person is feeling, try to understand their point of view.
3 *Do not try to change the others' identity or style of behaviour*. You will get better results if you adjust the way in which you respond than if you try to change the other person's behaviour.
4 *Express your own point of view carefully*. If you disagree you must say so clearly and assertively. You may have to move your position if the majority do not agree with you nevertheless; if you disagree, it is important that you state your opinion clearly and concisely.

Activity 56

Consider a conflict that you have had with a colleague at work. Analyse the conflict using the following questions as a prompt:
    What was the conflict about?
Using Kindler's model, analyse why the conflict occurred.
What was the outcome of the conflict?
Could you have handled the situation better if you had used Kindler's four principles for resolving conflict?
What have you learnt from this activity?

Summary

In this chapter we have looked at many issues around working with other people. It is vital that you have constructive working relationships with all your colleagues. You are particularly responsible for the quality of relationships within your team. We have considered the importance of supporting members of your workteam by counselling when necessary. We have considered the need for rules at work, disciplinary and grievance procedures and touched on the role of unions in the workplace and the increasing move towards employee participation at work. Finally we have examined conflict at work and considered why conflict arises and methods of dealing with conflict at work. Working with others is a crucial part of a team leader's role. Dealing with the issues that we have covered in this chapter in a professional way will enhance your performance at work.

Review and discussion questions

1 What is the difference between advice and counselling?
2 Give three examples of behaviour in a member of your team which may indicate the need for a counselling interview.
3 List the objectives of a counselling interview
4 How do you demonstrate 'empathy' with the speaker?
5 Why are rules at work necessary?
6 Why is it important for an organization to have a grievance procedure?
7 ACAS have set out the essential features of a good disciplinary procedure. What are these?
8 What is the difference between misconduct and gross misconduct?
9 What types of penalties or punishment may be the result of a disciplinary hearing, where the employee is found to be at fault?
10 What actions must you take to follow-up a disciplinary interview?
11 Draw a flow chart illustrating a typical grievance procedure.
12 What must you do to prepare for a grievance interview?
13 What is the role of trade unions?
14 Give four examples of employee participation.
15 What kind of benefits can be gained from conflict?
16 What are the four main causes of conflict according to Kindler?
17 List Kindler's four principles for resolving conflict.
18 Your manager has expressed some irritation whilst talking to you about Louise, one of the members of your section. Louise has recently broken-up with her partner, and is very distressed. 'My advice was to pull herself together and

get on with her work, but she doesn't seem to have taken any notice,' she says. Do you think your manager could have handled the situation better? How should she have dealt with the situation?

Case study 1 You are a team leader working in a building society.

Graham joined your staff straight from school some nine months ago. He is a quick learner and does his job increasingly well. However, he dresses in a slovenly manner and, even when he can be persuaded to wear appropriate dress, he does so grudgingly and his clothes and grooming are not up to standard. Despite frequent reminders, his appearance is still not acceptable. Your manager has asked you to 'deal with it as a disciplinary matter'. What are the informal and formal options open to discipline Graham? Suggest the actions you would choose to take, and why.

Case study 2 You have discovered, to your distress, that one of your operators, Linda, is about to invoke the grievance procedure against the management for failing to call a male member of staff to task on accusations of sexual harassment. Linda has now approached you for support. She has not spoken to you before, having been too shy. What part can you, as a team leader, play in the steps to be taken as part of the grievance procedure?

Work-based assignment

C15.2

Various activities in this chapter have asked you to obtain copies of your organization's rules, disciplinary and grievance procedures.

Conduct a review of this documentation, and your procedures, by answering the questions below. (If you do not have published rules and/or disciplinary and grievance procedures write a brief report to your manager suggesting why these should be introduced.)

Rules	Are they written down?	
	Are they easy to understand?	
	Are they accessible? Does everyone know where to find them?	
	What areas do they cover?	
	Do staff receive appropriate training to help them implement the grievance procedure?	
	Are they regularly reviewed?	
Disciplinary procedure	Do they follow the guidelines set out in paragraph 10 of the ACAS Code of Practice?	
	Do they clearly state what constitutes gross misconduct?	

Disciplinary procedure *continued*	Are they used responsibly to help an employee who is not performing effectively to improve performance?	
	Do staff receive appropriate training to help them implement the disciplinary procedure?	
Grievance procedure	Is the procedure clearly described?	
	Are there time limits for each stage of the procedure?	
	Is the procedure used in a responsible way to resolve disputes that cannot be resolved by any other means?	
	Do staff receive appropriate training to help them implement the grievance procedure?	

12 Managing change

Learning objectives

On completion of this chapter you will be able to:

- understand the importance of developing the skills to manage change
- identify the external forces which drive internal changes
- appreciate why people resist change
- understand the positive aspects of change
- describe the stages of introducing change
- use techniques to overcome resistance to change
- create an atmosphere in which change is accepted and even welcomed.

Introduction

The management of change has become one of the most important aspects of a manager's job. You will only be a good manager if you can manage change. The only certainty today is that everything is constantly changing. You need to have the skills and knowledge to manage change effectively. Management today is about responsiveness, flexibility and adaptability. Our society has adapted rapidly over the past 200 years from an agricultural society in which most people lived and worked in rural communities, to a modern industrial society where most of us live in cities and work in factories or offices. In the past, businesses relied on manual effort. A successful business today relies on high quality service and knowledge.

Changes are taking place all the time. Gradual change of this type happens slowly. It is not introduced as a major change programme and so it tends not to be specifically managed. An example of this type of gradual change might be the regular upgrading of the IT (information technology) packages that are used in organizations. On the other hand, sudden and major changes are immediately noticeable; it is generally recognized that major changes need to be planned for and managed. An example of this type of change would be the introduction of a new way of working, such as the introduction of multi-skilled workteams. Other examples are organization restructures, take-overs; an example of change on a smaller scale is moving work premises. It does not matter if the change is big or small, you will improve the chances of it being successful if you manage it.

Gradual change should be managed as well: in the example above, the gradual updating of IT packages. It is important that managers take an overview of what is happening and that there is an overall strategy for managing the use of IT within the organization.

Change affects the people who work in the organization. Most people find it difficult to change; they find change disturbing and threatening. It will help you, when introducing changes, to understand the bigger picture as to why the changes are taking place, how the introduction of change affects individuals and to look at some suggestions regarding how to introduce the change as effectively as possible.

Successful managers need to manage change thoughtfully and positively. This is particularly important as the rate of change is accelerating and you will need to spend more of your time dealing with issues around the management of change.

Forces for change

There are many external factors that lead to change within organizations. We will look at these now. The list that follows gives some of the factors, with some examples, of the forces that shape both the rate of change and the type of change that people and organizations have to deal with today.

- *Technological* – the rate of technological change is greater now than at any time in the past, for example, advances in IT.
- *Social* – the workforce has changed substantially over recent years; there are more educational opportunities, increased part-time working, changes in family lifestyles and an emphasis on equal opportunities.
- *Legal* – legal or tax changes affecting products or services.
- *Economic* – economic growth or recession, new market opportunities, deregulation.
- *Educational* – there has been a knowledge explosion with many new books and an increasing number of people undertaking some form of education. With this knowledge explosion, knowledge quickly becomes outdated or obsolete.

Activity 57

Complete the table below, giving an example of a recent change for each of the forces of change that has impacted upon your organization.

Force for change	A recent example
Technological	
Social	
Legal	
Economic	
Educational	

Resistance to change

Despite the fact that change is potentially positive, change is often resisted by people in organizations. Resistance to change can take many forms. The reasons that people resist change include the following:

- *Fear of the unknown* – changes which confront people with the unknown tend to cause anxiety and fear. Individuals are afraid of failing in their new role. They fear losing their jobs.
- *Security in the past* – people find a sense of security in the past and often wish to retain old and comfortable ways.
- *Status and position* – changes are often seen as altering the formal and informal status hierarchy.
- *Uncertainty* – the capacity to deal with uncertainty and ambiguity differs from one person to another. For some people, changing tried and trusted methods for something new and strange is traumatic.

- *Economic implications* – people are often concerned that change will reduce their pay or other rewards.
- *Inconvenience* – if it is perceived that introducing the change will result in inconvenience or more control over work, there will be resistance.
- *Habit* – habits are comforting and provide security. 'Old habits die hard'. It is difficult to get people to change their habits.
- *Loss of colleagues/workmates* – people do not like to move away from their working group.

Activity 58

Consider a recent change that took place in your organization that impacted on you. Analyse how you felt about that change by completing the table below.

A brief description of the change:

An analysis of my feelings about the change – a description of my feelings regarding resistance to the change

Fear of the unknown

Security in the past

Status and position

Uncertainty

Economic implications

Inconvenience

Habit

Loss of colleagues/workmates

ASSESSING AND DEVELOPING YOUR OWN PERFORMANCE

The positive aspects of change

In completing the activity above you reflected on how you felt about a change that was being introduced. You will have experienced the fears that everybody else does when change is introduced. You need to be positive when 'selling' the benefits of change to your team. Even if you have some personal doubts or worries you must not let your team know about these. Remember change often brings many positive benefits.

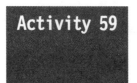

Activity 59

Reflect on the change that you analysed in Activity 58. What were the benefits of introducing the change that you analysed?

See Feedback section for answer to this activity.

The stages of introducing change

The model shown in Figure 12.1 suggests a step-by-step process that you can use for introducing change.

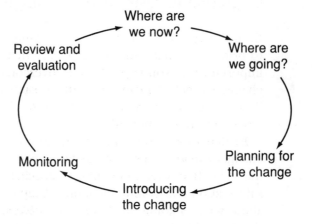

Figure 12.1
A step by step
process to
introducing change

Where are we now?

The first stage of the change process is to establish exactly where you are now, in relation to the change that is going to be brought in. You need to establish this information quite clearly so that you can map the journey from where you are now to where you want to be. This information can also be used to reinforce the improvements that will be made by introducing the change.

Where are we going?

You then need to establish exactly where you are going, what you want to achieve by introducing the change, when you want to achieve it by and how you will know when you have successfully achieved what you have set out to do. It would be helpful to set some SMART objectives, as described in Chapter 1, that you can use to measure your achievements against and so that you know when you have achieved what you set out to achieve.

Planning for the change

You are now ready to draw up the plans for introducing the change. You will need to include in your plans the methods that you will use for overcoming resistance to change.

Overcoming resistance to change

Even though people tend to resist change, it will be your job to bring in changes and to make sure that they work. It is important that you know how to overcome resistance to change so that you can deal with resistance in your workteam. When trying to overcome resistance to change in your workteam, remember PIE:

Participation - encourage your team to participate in the change. *Involve* your team, as far as you can do, in decisions that will affect them, encourage participation.

Information and communication - keep everyone informed about what is going on. *Listen to problems and deal with them quickly.* Ensure that your team have sufficient information to understand the need for the change.

Enthusiasm and education - ensure that your team know and understand the reasons for the changes, ensure that they have the right *training* and information to enable them to cope with the change. If you are enthusiastic about the change, your workteam will be more enthusiastic about it. Give your team members the *support* they need to make the transition.

Activity 60

Consider a small change that you need to implement in your section. Use the chart below to note down what you can do under the PIE model to introduce the change as smoothly as possible.

Details of the change that I need to introduce:		
Participation	How I will encourage participation	
Information	How I will ensure that people are informed	
Enthusiasm and education	How I will ensure that the change is brought in enthusiastically and the team are trained to deal with the change	

Successfully introducing change

A three-step model for successfully introducing change has been proposed by Kurt Lewin. You might wish to use this model to help you when planning to introduce change. The model will help you to understand the process and can be used for all types of change. The model has three phases: unfreezing, changing and refreezing.

Unfreezing

Before changes can be successfully introduced into the organization, Lewin says that the structures, procedures and norms that are about the 'old' way of doing things have to be unfrozen. This results in an awareness that things need to be changed. This is done by:

- shocking people into the realization of the need for change
- confronting people with the dangers of not changing
- spelling out the benefits of the change
- explaining the nature of the change needed
- describing the methods planned to achieve the change
- dealing with the needs of those affected, by counselling about unresolved worries
- explaining the ways that progress will be planned and monitored
- getting participation in the process.

Changing

The unfreezing process encourages people to consider alternative ways; it is at this stage that the actual change can take place by:

- defining the problems
- identifying the solutions
- possibly using a pilot project to identify any problems and learn from snags
- drawing up an action plan
- ensuring that everyone is clear about their responsibilities
- implementing the solution
- handling problems as they arise
- training in new skills.

Refreezing

This is the phase during which change is stabilised and integrated into the rest of the system. Team leaders need to ensure that:

- complaints are handled positively and quickly
- successes are highlighted

- changed behaviour is rewarded
- managers set a good example
- relationships are built and rebuilt where necessary
- systems are consolidated
- everybody involved owns the change.

This model has several benefits:

- it can be easily understood
- it is possible to recognize the stage of the change that has been reached
- the same process can be used for all changes and people get used to using it
- it encourages discussion of the process and impact of change, throughout the period of the change.

Monitoring

It is essential to continually monitor progress against plans to see how you are doing. You will have a plan for introducing the change. You need to keep a watch on how things are going so that you can make adjustments to the plan if difficulties occur. There will be certain key milestones in the plan, i.e. specific dates by which things must be done before you can move on to the next stage. You will need to continuously monitor what is actually happening against the plan to ensure that you are still on course. You need to be aware of issues that may develop within the team and try to maintain the momentum and enthusiasm by dealing with problems as they arise and keeping your team informed at all stages. As with most plans, it is unlikely that everything will go just right. You will need to readjust your original plan in the light of slippages owing to unforeseen events.

Review and evaluation

A vital stage in any plan, in fact any activity that you carry out, is the review and evaluation stage. It is a good idea to build into the plan formal reviews. That is, certain dates when you take some time to review the progress to date. You may wish to do this in a team meeting. A review is a more formal method of monitoring. You will definitely want a review meeting at the end of the project.

When the change has been successfully implemented you need to take time out to evaluate the process. What difficulties did you encounter and why? What monitoring processes need to be put in place now to ensure that things run smoothly? What else needs doing now? What have you learnt from the process of introducing the change?

Activity 61

Use the change that you analysed in Activity 60. How will you review and evaluate the change?

Summary

In this chapter we have considered, in some detail, how you can successfully introduce change at work. We have looked at the external factors that drive changes within your organization and introduced a step-by-step approach that you can use as a model when introducing change at work. Remember that one of the most important things that you must be able to do to be a good team leader is to manage change successfully.

Review and discussion questions

1 Why is it important for team leaders to be able to manage change?
2 List the five forces that influence organizational change.
3 Why do people resist change?
4 What are the benefits of change at work?
5 List the five stages for introducing change.
6 How can a team leader overcome resistance to change?
7 Briefly explain Kurt Lewin's three-step model for introducing change.
8 Why is it essential to continuously monitor the change process?
9 What questions must you answer when evaluating the introduction of a change?
10 Discuss some of the major changes confronting your organization. How well is change planned, implemented and managed in your organization?

ASSESSING AND DEVELOPING YOUR OWN PERFORMANCE

Case study

Williams & Co was a small firm, a retail outlet selling computer hardware and software, mainly to individuals and small- to medium-sized companies. Until recently the business was owned and managed by Mr Williams, who employed 30 staff, many of whom had worked for the organization for several years; some of the staff had worked at Williams since the business was started 10 years ago. Mr Williams has recently sold the business to a large national retailer, Quickcompute. They intend to keep the business open but have introduced many changes to ensure that the outlet that they have taken over meets Quickcompute standards.

All the staff have been issued with bright new uniforms. The work patterns have been altered and so they are no longer working in the teams that they have worked with for years. The shop has been refurbished and the staff facilities improved. All of the staff have had a pay rise to bring their salaries in line with their counterparts in the rest of Quickcompute.

The regional manager, Geoff Jones, is bemused. All the changes have been introduced very quickly and yet sales have fallen and the staff seem to be demotivated and, in his words, 'ungrateful'. Geoff says, 'I can't understand them. They've got better working conditions than they've ever had, and yet they are not performing well. We took care of all the shop refurbishment for them. They've not had to think about anything and yet sales have fallen substantially. I can see that their heart isn't in the job'.

Where do you think Quickcompute have gone wrong? What can they do now to improve the situation? How would you advise Quickcompute to deal with take-overs in the future?

Work-based assignment

C12.1

1 Describe a change that has recently been introduced in your organization. Choose a change that has had an impact on the way that your team and/or you work.
2 How was the change introduced?
3 What impact did the change have on you and your team?
4 How did you and your team feel about the change?
5 Suggest how the implementation of the change could have been improved.

Feedback

Activity 3   Your answer might have included some of the following types of planning activities that team leaders are often involved in:

- planning work
- planning staffing schedules
- planning the use of machines and other physical resources
- planning budgets
- planning maintenance of plant
- planning training.

Activity 4   Your answer may have included some of the following methods:

- talking to staff
- holding team briefings
- staff meetings
- by telephone
- meetings
- writing memos
- signs
- giving instructions.

A good team leader will spend a great deal of time communicating with the team.

Activity 5   You might have included some of the following activities in your answer:

- maintaining and checking production/work records
- walking around to check how things are going
- checking quality
- checking safety standards
- ensuring everybody starts work on time
- deciding work priorities.

Activity 12

Your answer might have included some of the following roles:

- daughter/son
- parent
- partner
- your role in the team that you work with
- member of a quality improvement team
- roles that you have outside work which form part of your social life.

Activity 22

Closed question	Rephrased into an open question
Did you enjoy your last job?	What aspects of your last job did you enjoy?
Do you feel you learnt a lot while you were at school?	What did you learn at school that has been particularly valuable?
Were you attracted to this job because of the salary?	What attracted you to this job?
Do you feel you are qualified for this job?	What qualifications do you have that make you suitable for this job?
Wouldn't you say that you've changed jobs a lot?	Why have you changed jobs so often?
Have you ever had a personality clash with people in that company?	What sort of difficult situations have you experienced with colleagues?
Were you closely supervised in your last job?	How much freedom did you have to manage and make decisions in your last job?
I've heard that it's a terrible company to work for. Is that true?	What is the company like to work for?
We need someone who can handle a lot of pressure. Can you do that?	What experience do you have of working under pressure?

Activity 25   Everyone will come up with a different set of names for this activity. There are great historical leaders, Churchill, Hitler, Napoleon and more modern-day leaders, Gary Lineker, Alex Ferguson, Richard Branson, Anita Roddick, Sir John Harvey Jones.

Activity 33   Your answer might have included some of the following:

Type of training	Advantages	Problems
Skill practice	Cheap; not in a 'real' situation so trainee cannot make a serious mistake	Time-consuming
Demonstration	Cheap; avoids passing on bad habits	Encourages dependence; time consuming
Projects	Live projects – very useful to the organization	Problem fitting in project with normal work load
Sitting with 'Nellie'	Cheap; easy; passes on the skills of an experienced person	Lack of control by the supervisor; Nellie might not be good at training; bad work habits might be passed on; a nuisance and interruption to Nellie's work
Coaching	One-to-one attention; focused; concentrates on real work; low cost	Success depends on team leader's skill as a coach
Mentoring	One-to-one attention; focused on individual's needs; work focus; low cost	Success depends on skill of mentor; time consuming for mentor
Delegation	Supervisor delegates own work and so benefits from free time	Team leader retains responsibility
Secondment	Trainee understands the organization as a whole; real situation	Trainee away from the workplace

Activity 37
You may have listed some of the following:

- your learning will meet your own specific needs
- it will lead to better performance at work
- enhanced career prospects
- greater confidence
- it will be cost effective because it will definitely meet your specific needs
- you will be more enthusiastic and motivated
- you will constantly seek out learning opportunities
- you can work at your own pace using a method that suits you best.

Activity 44
The answers are:

1 Assertive
2 Aggressive
3 Submissive

Activity 46

1 Parent
2 Child
3 Child
4 Adult
5 Adult
6 Child.

Activity 47
The work which made you feel satisfied probably gave you the opportunity to do some of the following:

- do interesting work
- be good at what you do
- be appreciated for what you do
- do challenging work
- take some responsibility.

Activity 48

1 Self-fulfilment and security
2 Status/ego and self-fulfilment
3 Security
4 Belonging and status/ego
5 Self-fulfilment
6 Self-fulfilment

     7 Self-fulfilment
     8 Self-fulfilment and status/ego
     9 Belonging and status/ego
    10 Self-fulfilment.

Activity 49

Your answer might have included some of the following classic signs of demotivation:

- poor time-keeping
- high absenteeism
- apathy
- indifference
- complaints or disagreements about tasks
- stolen minutes of inactivity, such as unnecessary inter-office visits, excessive loo visits, extended breaks, magazine reading, phone chats
- grievances
- lack of cooperation
- slow work rate
- resistance to change.

Activity 55

You might have included some of the following in your list:

- conflict can result in good ideas
- if conflict is brought out into the open and dealt with, grievances/disagreements will not fester and cause discontent and resentment.
- if team members are worried or concerned about something, the freedom to confidently express their concerns will allay their fears.
- if team members are able to express their concerns a better, compromise, solution may result.

Activity 59

Some of the benefits that you listed might have been:

- more interesting work – a change often means that people's jobs change. Very often this can lead to more interesting work which can lead to a new enthusiasm for the job
- improved career prospects – if you introduce the change enthusiastically and successfully, your chances for developing your own career may improve
- an opportunity to learn new skills and so develop yourself – change may mean that you need to learn new skills that will add value to you as a person, give you the opportunity for self-development and provide you with a new challenge.

References

Adair, J. (1979) *Action-Centred Leadership*, Gower

Adair, J (1984) *The Skills of Leadership*, Gower

Belbin, R.M. (1981) *Management Teams: Why They Succeed or Fail*, Butterworth-Heinemann

Belbin, R.M. (1993) *Team Roles at Work*, Butterworth-Heinemann

Berne, E. (1966) *Games People Play*, Penguin

Blake, R.R. and Mouton, J.S. (1985) *The Managerial Grid III*, Gulf Publishing Company

British Institute of Management (now The Institute of Management) (1977) *Employee Participation – The Way Ahead*

Deal, T.E. and Kennedy, A.A. (1982) *Corporate Cultures: The Rites and Rituals of Corporate Life*, Penguin

Drucker, P.F. (1989) *The Practice of Management*, Butterworth-Heinemann

Eysenck, H.J. (1960) *The Structure of Human Personality*, Methuen

Eysenck, H.J. (1973) *Eysenck on Extroversion*, Crosby, Lockwood Staples

French, J.R.P. and Raven, B. (1968) The bases of social power. In *Group Dynamics: Research and Theory*, 3rd edn (ed. D. Cartwright and A.F. Zander) Harper and Row

Frazer, J.M. (1978) *Employment Interviewing*, 5th edn, Macdonald and Evans

Handy, C.B. (1993) *Understanding Organisations*, 4th edn, Penguin

Herzberg, F., Mausner, B. and Synderman, B.B. (1959) *The Motivation to Work*, 2nd edn, Chapman and Hall

Herzberg, F. (1974) *Work and the Nature of Man*, Granada Publishing

Honey, P. and Mumford, A. (1992) *The Manual of Learning Styles*, 3rd edn, Peter Honey Publications (this incorporates the Learning Styles Questionnaire which is referred to in Activity 38, p.132

Industrial Relations Services (1995) *Employment Trends 591. Discipline at Work – the Practice*

Kindler, H.S. (1988) *Managing Disagreement Constructively*, Kogan Page

Kolb, D.A. (1985) *Experiential Learning: Experience as the Source of Learning and Development*, Prentice-Hall

Kolb, D.A., Rubin, I.M. and McIntyre, J.M. (1984) *Organisational Psychology: An Experiential Approach to Organisational Behaviour*, Prentice Hall

Lewin, K. (1951) *Field Theory in Social Science*, Harper and Row

Maslow, A.H. (1943) A theory of human motivation. *Psychological Review*, **50**, 370–96

Maslow, A.H. (1987) *Motivation and Personality*, 3rd edn, Harper and Row

McGregor, D. (1987) *The Human Side of Enterprise*, Penguin

Mullins, L.J. (1996) *Management and Organisational Behaviour*, 4th edn, Pitman

Mintzberg, H. (1973) *The Nature of Managerial Work*, Harper and Row

Porter, L.W. and Lawler, E.E. (1968) *Managerial Attributes and Performance*, Irwin

Rodyer, A. (1970) *The Seven Point Plan*, 3rd edn. Originally devised for the National Institute of Industrial Psychology; now available from the National Foundation for Educational Research

Roethlisberger, F.J. and Dickson, W.J. (1939) *Management and the Worker*, Harvard University Press

Tannenbaum, R. and Schmidt, W.H. (1973) How to choose a leadership pattern. *Harvard Business Review*, May–June, 162–75, 178–80

Taylor, F.W. (1947) *Scientific Management*, Harper and Row

Tuckman, B.W. (1965) Development sequence in small groups. *Psychological Bulletin*, **63**, 384–99

Vroom, V.H. (1964) *Work and Motivation*, John Wiley

Further Reading

ACAS (1997) *Discipline at Work* (Advisory Handbook)

ACAS (XXXX) *Code of Practice 1 Disciplinary Practice and Procedures in Employment*

ACAS (1997) *Employee Appraisal* (Advisory booklet)

ACAS (1997) *Recruitment and Induction* (Advisory booklet)

NEBS Management (1997) *Appraising Performance* (Super Series 3), Butterworth-Heinemann

NEBS Management (1997) *Becoming More Effective* (Super Series 3), Butterworth-Heinemann

NEBS Management (1997) *Commitment to Equality* (Super Series 3), Butterworth-Heinemann

NEBS Management (1997) *Delegating Effectively* (Super Series 3), Butterworth-Heinemann

NEBS Management (1997) *Delivering Training* (Super Series 3), Butterworth-Heinemann

NEBS Management (1997) *How Organizations Work* (Super Series 3), Butterworth-Heinemann

NEBS Management (1997) *Leading Your Team* (Super Series 3), Butterworth-Heinemann

NEBS Management (1997) *Managing with Authority* (Super Series 3), Butterworth-Heinemann

NEBS Management (1997) *Managing Lawfully – People and Employment* (Super Series 3), Butterworth-Heinemann

NEBS Management (1997) *Managing Time* (Super Series 3), Butterworth-Heinemann

NEBS Management (1997) *Managing Tough Times* (Super Series 3), Butterworth-Heinemann

NEBS Management (1997) *Motivating People* (Super Series 3), Butterworth-Heinemann

NEBS Management (1997) *Planning Training and Development* (Super Series 3), Butterworth-Heinemann

NEBS Management (1997) *Securing the Right People* (Super Series 3), Butterworth-Heinemann

NEBS Management (1997) *Working in Teams* (Super Series 3), Butterworth-Heinemann

Index